Do-It-Yourself
Roofing
and Siding

Do-It-Yourself Roofing and Siding

MAX ALTH

HAWTHORN BOOKS, INC.
Publishers / NEW YORK
A Howard & Wyndham Company

All photographs and drawings not credited to others are
by Max and Simon Alth.

TO
Char,
Syme,
Misch,
Mike,
Arabella, and
Mendle

Contents

Foreword

This book will show you how to side and re-side your home with aluminum and plastic siding and will also show you how to roof and reroof your home with asphalt shingles and asphalt roll roofing.

If you have never done any mechanical work, roofing and siding may appear to be complicated and difficult. They are not. If you can use a ruler, a hammer, and a saw, you can roof and side because both these trades are to a great extent foolproof. They require very little experience and skill.

Applying roofing and siding is not like laying bricks, to make one comparison. Whereas the mason must exercise some judgment in laying a brick in mortar, nothing is dependent on the roofing and siding mechanic's visual judgment. Siding and roofing are placed against a mark or line and, in the case of siding, most of it is fitted into a slot. There is no guesswork.

The major difference between the beginner's and the expert's work in siding and roofing is speed. The beginner will take much longer. However, there is no pressing need to finish siding or roofing within any time limit. The work can be stretched over any number of weekends.

And even if as a beginner you take twice as long as the experts, the money to be saved is still worth your time because it can be as much as 63 percent of that asked by a reputable contractor. Since a roofing or siding job can run to several thousand dollars, the saving will be considerable.

At the same time, in fair weather, the work is not unpleasant. And if the weather is or becomes foul, you can always wait for another day. I always do.

Acknowledgment

I wish to acknowledge my appreciation for the technical assistance and encouragement given me by Joseph Nichols, President, Buy Rite Siding, Inc., 517 Hunter Mountain Road, Naugatuck, Connecticut.

PART ONE

Siding

1

All About Siding

Modern wood-frame homes are literally constructed of 2- by 4-inch-thick lengths of lumber called studs, spaced a distance apart and nailed together to make the walls. To cover the spaces between the studs and to hold them rigid, the exterior of the wall is covered with sheathing. This may consist of fibrous, fireproof sheets; exterior Sheetrock (plasterboard); 1- by-8-inch boards; or sheets of plywood. When economy is the controlling factor, plywood may be the only external cover placed on the building frame.

When better sense prevails, the sheathing is covered with external siding. This may consist of shingles made of asbestos, asphalt, wood, or even metal. Siding is also manufactured in strip form from wood, aluminum, plywood, hardboard, steel, and plastic. Applied to the sheathing in a vertical position the strips of siding are called vertical siding, and may be further defined as lap siding, or board-and-batten siding. Strip siding designed for horizontal use divides into lap siding and clapboard or is made to look like these basic types of siding. There are also variations that are made from all of the materials mentioned except wood. These variations include siding that looks like stucco and siding strips that resemble wood shingles.

3

Any of these sidings may be used on new construction. Any of these sidings can be used atop old, in-place siding. They can even be used atop a masonry wall. However, for many reasons metal (aluminum and steel) and plastic strip siding is the best to use on new work and especially on old work. And of the three sidings that fall into this "best" category, aluminum siding is the most popular. Aluminum siding has been used for more than thirty years, and so far, more than ten million homes have been sided with this metal. Plastic siding follows weakly behind, with steel siding still further behind. All in all, six times more homes are being sided and re-sided with aluminum than with any other siding.

FORMED STRIP VERSUS OTHER SIDINGS

Easy installation. Strip siding, applied either horizontally or vertically, is much easier to install than shingles of any type mainly because the strip is larger and you cover more wall surface with each piece. In addition the formed strip siding we are discussing is manufactured with what may be termed a built-in guide that automatically holds exposure constant. (Exposure is the surface area of each piece of siding, whether it is strip or shingle, that is visible.) The length of the strips also makes them easier to install because it is usually easier to hold a long strip horizontal or vertical than it is to hold small rectangles to a line.

Formed strip siding is easier to install than wood strip siding and shingles because formed siding is part of a "system." Formed siding is not simply applied to the walls of the building like wood siding. Formed siding is held in place by preformed channels. Whereas clapboard, a type of wood strip siding, must fit tightly against the house trim, formed strip siding fits inside a channel nailed to the trim. As a result cutting errors of as much as ⅜ inch remain hidden within the channel.

Permanence. All the three formed sidings mentioned will last the life of the house. Both asphalt and hardboard siding deteriorate with time. Both have to be replaced eventually unless you paint the hardboard as assiduously as you should paint wood. The asphalt shingle gradually loses its mineral surface, and the basic black substrate shows through. Shortly thereafter the shingle curls up. Asbestos does not deteriorate with time, but its porous surface is a natural collector of dirt, and whatever color is applied to the shingle soon disappears. As a result, the homeowner has either some very serious scrubbing or painting to do if his or her home is to look clean and well kept.

Formed strip siding does not lose its appearance nearly as fast and can easily be washed clean with a little soap and water. The reason is the materials used and the method of manufacture.

The paints used are similar to automobile paints and are baked on. Formed aluminum siding can be purchased with paint warranteed for as long as forty years. Plastic siding is one color or tone clear through. It won't lose its color, although the color does fade with time and the siding's surface may roughen slightly.

Appearance. None of the three formed sidings can be differentiated from their wood counterparts at a moderate distance. It is only when you come close enough to touch the siding that the difference becomes obvious. Wood siding is butted up against the door and window frames, whereas formed metal and plastic siding are not. They are usually mounted within channels. Formed strip siding does not become rough and striated the way the surface of wood becomes with the passage of time, especially when the homeowner delays too long between paintings. Formed strip siding can be had with a wood-grain surface texture. This texture does not vary with age.

Fire protection. Both aluminum and steel formed strip sidings are completely fireproof—naturally, they are metals. The polyvinyl chloride (PVC) plastic presently used for making siding can burn. However, it is difficult to ignite. Its flash ignition temperature is 700 degrees Fahrenheit as compared to 445 degrees for paper and

Applying 8-inch aluminum siding to the gable end of a split-level home. The siding is placed atop "core board," a new type of siding support material consisting of a ¼-inch thick layer of styrofoam between two sheets of heavy paper. It has an R rating of about 1.6. *Courtesy Buy Rite Siding, Inc.*

500 degrees for Douglas fir. Also, PVC burns very poorly, much like a pile of wet leaves. When burning, it produces hydrogen chloride, carbon dioxide, and carbon monoxide. Hydrogen chloride is a noxious gas that can be quickly sensed at concentrations that are not considered to be acutely toxic. Carbon monoxide is a deadly poison that is very dangerous because it has no characteristic odor.

Temperatures, such as caused by a neighboring fire, that are too low to ignite PVC but hot enough to blister and char ordinary paint will cause plastic siding to sag and even melt.

Thus when you side your home with either of the metal sidings, you are reducing the chance of your home being set on fire by an external source of heat. While it is true that most home fires originate within the building and that most of the damage is due to smoke and smoke inhalation, it is still good to know that a brush fire or a fire in a neighboring building will be unlikely to set your home on fire or damage it severely. At the present writing, insur-

Job completed. Ladders and scaffold removed. *Courtesy Buy Rite Siding, Inc.*

ance companies will not grant a lower fire insurance premium rate to wooden homes when they are sided with metal, but it is not inconceivable that they will, since metal siding does lower the incidence of fire.

COMPARATIVE COSTS

Initial costs. The following price list is only approximate and does not include or consider different gauge metals, styles, and so on. The prices do, however, include an approximation of the associate materials you will need with the different types of siding. For example, the aluminum siding figure includes starter strips, nails, channels, and so on. The figures do not include unavoidable waste that results when you have to cut the siding to fit into odd spaces.

Approximate Cost of Siding per Square Foot plus Accessory Material*

Aluminum	$.85
Asbestos	.30
Steel	.58
Plastic	.65
Wood strip	.80
Wood shingle	.70

(Figures do not include waste)

Quick pricing. Measure the total area of the exterior of your home in square feet. (This is discussed in detail in Chapter 3.) Do not subtract the doors, windows, and other openings. Multiply this figure by the figure given on the preceding list. By not deducting for the openings in the figure, you more or less account for the waste that always results from cutting. Typically, a ranch house will take a total of 1,700 square feet. A colonial will require about 2,300 square feet.

Do not try to estimate the cost of materials from any bid you may receive on the job from a contractor. If you take the trouble to secure a number of bids, you will find that they wander all over and that it is not unusual to have one contractor ask two and even three times what another contractor asks. You may also receive some very low bids. These may simply be mistakes or they may be "crying" bids. The contractor knowingly bids much too low. Then in the middle of the job he cries that he has erred and if he is not paid more money, he will be forced to quit right then and there.

So even though a fair bid should be approximately three times the cost of the materials alone, don't work backward from any bid to find the cost of materials required. Chances are you will not get the correct answer.

---

* Figures reflect average prices as of summer 1977.

Fuel savings. Formed strip siding has a natural air pocket behind it. Even when no additional insulation is used, these air pockets serve as insulators and provide much more insulation than asbestos or asphalt shingles and almost as much insulation as wood siding of a thickness equal to the air pocket. Wood siding ½ inch thick has an R rating of 0.81. (The higher the R rating, the greater the material's resistance to the flow of heat and the greater its insulating properties.) Aluminum siding with nothing behind it has an R rating of 0.75. Plastic has a fractionally higher rating. When you put polystyrene foam and foil behind aluminum siding, its rating goes up to 2.50. That is as much as 30 inches of stone masonry or 12 inches of brick.

The actual quantity of fuel you can expect to save by re-siding your home with insulated, formed strip siding depends on many factors. However, you can be certain that no matter how well your home may presently be insulated, you can reduce your annual fuel bill by 10 to 20 percent.

Since you will be heating your home forever and there appears to be no stopping the rising cost of fuel, you can readily appreciate just how much money can be saved over the years. Typically, a poorly insulated home in the Boston area will realize an annual fuel saving of about $150 when it is sided with insulated, formed strip siding.

Cooling costs. Few homeowners considering re-siding ever think about the potential reduction of air-conditioning power usage. But the same insulation that reduces the outflow of heat in the winter will reduce the inflow of heat in the summer. The metal sidings are particularly good in this respect because the metal reflects much of the radiant energy striking the building. Although there are no specific figures, I estimate that savings could be from 2 to 5 percent over the summer months. A small percentage, but it continues indefinitely.

Painting. When you re-side, you avoid the cost and labor of painting for as many years as the paint remains bright and fresh on the siding. Since siding manufacturers are willing to warranty their sidings for as many as forty years—and experience has shown that the appearance of these sidings can indeed last this long and longer—it is not unreasonable to use this figure in our calculations.

If you decide to paint rather than re-side your house, and if you contract your paint job, you will probably pay about 60 cents per square foot of exterior wall surface. If you do your own work, your costs for paint and sundries will probably run 20 cents per square foot. If you do your own re-siding, your total cost for material—and this includes waste as well as accessory materials—will probably run about $1 per square foot. The contract rate for siding will probably run about $3 per square foot.

Summing up. To place all the figures into easy perspective, let us assume the outside of your home has 1,700 square feet of surface, exclusive of windows, doors, etc., and that it was constructed before 1950 and therefore was not insulated at all. (It was not until 1970 that insulation became common.) Furthermore, let us assume your home is in the Boston area. Now, to put this example into specific, but still approximate, figures:

Do-it-yourself aluminum or plastic siding at $1 per square foot	$1,700
Contract siding at $3 per square foot	5,100
Do-it-yourself painting (every four years) at 20 cents per square foot	340
Contract painting (every four years) at 60 cents per square foot	1,020
Heat savings per year	150

As you can see, when you re-side the house with aluminum or plastic, you will save $1,020 plus four times $150, or $1,620, in contract painting and heat every four years. Thus, in five years you will have paid off the cost of siding materials. If you contract the siding at the given figure, you will pay it off in a little less than thirteen years. That leaves twenty-seven years of savings, or $10,935, assuming you purchased the forty-year siding.

Naturally, if the cost of heating goes up, you will pay the job off sooner and save more.

QUESTIONS AND ANSWERS

Then what? What happens after the paint on the metal siding wears out? What happens after the plastic loses its color?

Aluminum takes paint beautifully. Just wash it clean and paint away. Steel siding also takes paint well where it has not been scratched. In those places where it has been scratched it is necessary to sandpaper the rust away and wash the bare metal with a mild acidlike vinegar or use a metal primer (you can spray it onto the bare spots). Then paint away.

Plastic does not take all paints well. However, when washed clean, it will take oil-based paint.

Can formed siding be damaged? Yes. If your favorite child takes a baseball bat to the side of the house, something distasteful will happen. The exact nature of the disaster will depend on the type of siding, its age, and its temperature at the time.

Plastic siding resists best of all when it is new and warm. If the impact is a fraction less than the plastic can withstand at the moment, it will rebound and no harm will be done. The vinyl plastic used for siding is like all plastics we know today. It is composed of long chains of molecules. With the passage of time and especially with exposure to sunlight, the plastic suffers time and ultraviolet degradation. The molecular chains shorten and the plastic becomes brittle. This is most pronounced when the plastic is cold.

Steel siding resists blows best because it is the strongest. However, a blow that may bounce off plastic may dent the steel a little.

Aluminum is the most easily damaged of the three, but its susceptibility to denting can be measurably decreased by using insulation behind it. At the same time, aluminum siding is the most easily repaired of the three.

Will the colors fade? Yes. With the passage of time and depending on the strength of the sun and local air conditions, the colors will fade. Of the brighter colors, green appears to be the most fugitive. The pale colors stand up best, with white changing the least because it degrades into a soft grey, which remains attractive.

Plastic sidings are only made in pastel shades and white. Proportionately, their colors change less than the painted panels. And since their colors are integral—run all the way through—it would seem that they should hold color best of all. They don't; the surface of the plastic changes, and their colors show age to the same degree as the other panels do.

Will the metal sidings attract lightning? This is an old carpenter's tale. Lightning strikes the highest object in the area. For example, the Empire State Building is struck by lightning thousands of times a year—without harm. Lower, nearby buildings are rarely struck by lightning.

It is accepted that the safest place to be in a lightning storm, other than a neighboring state, is within a metal enclosure such as an automobile or metal-sided building. Should lightning strike, it will run down the metal exterior and then to the ground.

It is not necessary to ground metal siding—to connect a heavy wire from the siding to a pipe driven into damp earth. Experience of over thirty years with more than ten million metal-sided homes has shown no need for grounding. Grounding of metal siding is not required by either BOCA (Building Officials and Code Administrators) or the National Fire Protection Association (which sets forth the National Electrical Code and the National Fire Code). However, there may still be a local grounding rule in your community. Check this out. Grounding is simple enough and can be done after the siding is installed.

PAYING FOR IT ALL

Re-siding, of course, is a home improvement and is therefore eligible for ordinary bank home-improvement loans and FHA/HUD Title 1 loans. The latter have to be checked out with the local FHA/HUD office. The rate is lower and therefore worth checking. The maximum loan is now up to $10,000 with twelve years to pay.

CLEANING

For best results wash your home's siding twice a year. Use any type of sponge or rag, a little mild detergent, and plenty of water. The easy way to do the job is to use one of those auto brushes that has a brush attached to a long, hollow handle. The garden hose is connected to the end of the handle. All you need do then is go over the surface of the siding lightly, just once. If the surface is very dirty, dissolve a little soap in water and spray it on with a garden sprayer; then wash it off with clear water.

A COMPARISON OF THE QUALITIES OF THE VARIOUS SIDINGS

	Aluminum	Hardboard	Steel	Vinyl Plastic
Weather and pollution resistant	Yes	Yes	Yes	Yes
Affected by sunlight	Finish only	Finish only	Finish only	Yes
Fade resistance	Good	Good	Good	Good
Quality control of color	Excellent	Fair	Excellent	Fair
Dent resistance	Medium	Medium	Medium	High
Becomes brittle with age	No	No	No	Yes
Can crack or break in cold weather	No	No	No	Yes
Need periodic cleaning	Yes	Yes	Yes	Yes
Colors available	Wide range	Wide range	Wide range	White and pastel only
Textures and patterns available	Smooth, embossed, and heavy textures and patterns	Smooth, embossed, shallow, and heavy textures and patterns	Heavy textures and embossed	Smooth finish and shallow textures
Matching and coordinating accessories (shutters, downspouts and gutters, window trim, soffit, etc.)	Aluminum accessories available	Wood and aluminum accessories generally used	Aluminum trim generally used	Aluminum trim generally used

Warp resistance	Excellent	Fair (tempered)	Excellent	Fair
Termite resistance	Excellent	Fair	Excellent	Excellent
Fire resistance	Excellent	Can burn	Excellent	Can burn
Red rust resistance	Excellent	Excellent	Fair	Excellent
Magnifies unevenness of wall	Very little	Very little	Very little	More than others
Warranties available	Generally 20–40 years	Variable	Generally 20–30 years	Generally 20–30 years
Moisture resistance	Excellent	Better than many wood products	Can rust if not properly coated	Excellent
Needs to be grounded	No	No	No	No
Attracts lightning	No	No	No	No
Can cause TV interference	Not a problem	Not a problem	Not a problem	Not a problem
Nails recommended for installing	Aluminum	Aluminum	Galvanized steel	Aluminum
Appearance of joints	Good	Fair	Good	Fair
Can be recycled	Always	Never	Sometimes	Never

Note: The above chart summarizes the best information available to us. Products obviously vary from manufacturer to manufacturer, and local regulations may affect the use or installation of certain products. *Courtesy the Aluminum Association, Inc.*

2

Aluminum Siding Materials

SOURCES OF SUPPLY

Aluminum siding is fabricated by perhaps a dozen companies who make it from aluminum strip provided by the aluminum-producing companies in this country and Canada.

Each siding fabricator produces a somewhat slightly different product and calls his siding and component parts a system. Except for minor details the systems are identical. However, you cannot assume that all parts of all systems are interchangeable. They probably are not.

All this should be no problem, since you will most likely and should purchase all the parts from one manufacturer. The point has been brought up for two reasons. First, in the discussion of installation that follows, the variations will be covered as if they are common to all systems. They are not. For example, Crown makes its siding to be joined by slipping the end of one panel beneath the adjoining panel and strengthening the joint with a backer strip when the panel is 8 inches wide. Luxaclad manufactures a joint mold—a kind of giant clip—to join their panel ends.

Second, you should be aware of the possibilitiy that old strips of siding offered by a friend or sold through an odd-lot bargain center may not fit what you have purchased elsewhere, let alone match its color.

It is advisable, of course, to use care in purchasing your material. Make certain you are dealing with a reputable supplier.* Make certain that he will accept undamaged returns. It is impossible to foretell accurately the exact quantity of material you will need. The general practice is to overpurchase and return the extra. In that way you can be certain all the colors will be exactly alike. An active dealer can always sell the small quantities for use on smaller projects. He won't be stuck with them.

SPECIFICATIONS FOR SIDING

Gauges, insulation and costs. Aluminum siding is manufactured in two gauges called thick and thin. The thick is 0.24 inch thick. The thin is 0.019 inch thick. The difference in price is small. The difference in insulating properties is insignificant. The handling properties are not. The thick is much easier to use. If you are planning to work alone, it is advisable to purchase the thick siding because, unless there are two pairs of hands, a strong wind can bend the light-gauge panels while you attempt to nail them in place. On the other hand, if you are seeking the best compromise between insulating efficiency and cost, the thin-gauge metal with the fiberboard backer is your best bet. The fiberboard makes the thin-gauge panel as stiff and as easily handled as the thicker-gauge panel without the backer.

Of course, the polystyrene, foil-backed panel offers the greatest degree of insulation. But it should be purchased in the thicker gauge when you are planning to work alone. The polystyrene doesn't add too much stiffness. In any event, if you are living fairly well up North, the polystyrene insulation will pay for itself in fuel savings in a relatively few years.

* You will find suppliers in the Yellow Pages of your phone book, listed under siding, roofing and siding, or building supplies. If you can't find a listing in the phone book, ask a nearby lumberyard.

Increased heating energy saving for $340 additional investment in polystyrene-insulated, foil-backed siding compared with plain foil-backed siding for 1,700-sq.-ft. wall surface on uninsulated house in Worcester, Mass., heated with heating oil costing 42¢/gal.

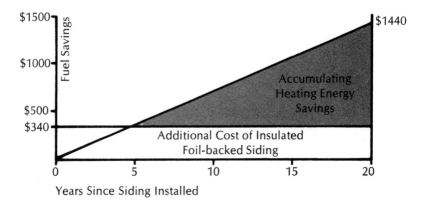

An example of the possible savings effected by using polystyrene-insulated aluminum panels with an R value of 2.50 in place of plain aluminum panels atop a layer of aluminum foil. Plain panels and foil alone have an R value of only 1.24. *Courtesy the Aluminum Association.*

Vertical and horizontal. In addition to being manufactured in two gauges, aluminum siding is made for both horizontal and vertical application. Although you can use either type in both positions, they will not look "right" if you do not position them as intended.

Styles and sizes. Horizontal siding is made by most of the companies in a number of styles and sizes. Most common are the 8-inch and the double–4-inch siding panels that give the appearance of similar width clapboard siding. The double-4 is somewhat stiffer than the 8 because of the fold along the center of the panel, which makes for the two-board appearance. There is also a clapboard-type siding with 5 inches of exposure and panels with two bevel edges, which give the appearance of being two strips of bevel-edge wood siding. These latter panels have 9 inches of exposure. Exposure, of course, is not the total width of the panel but the width of the panel area that is actually exposed to view and the weather.

Vertical siding is made in 10-, 12-, and 16-inch panels. These divide into board-and-batten and V-groove styles. The 16-inch board-and-batten is also made as a double-8. The V-groove pattern can also be had as a double-5 or a double-6, and the 16-inch-wide board-and-batten comes as a triple-5 and also with five 3-inch-wide indentations.

Colors and finishes. Aluminum siding is available in white, buff, brown, russet, green, gold, and many other colors or tones. Surface finishes vary from smooth, to textured by means of textured paint, textured by embossing, and textured by a combination of embossing and textured paint.

The paints are multilayered and baked on. And since the paint is on metal, there is no way for moisture to get behind the paint and cause it to blister, which can and does happen to paint on a wood base.

The paints are warranted for ten to as much as forty years. Naturally, the price of the siding varies to some related degree with

Three types of horizontal aluminum siding that are frequently used. Left to right: 8-inch textured with a polystyrene backer strip, double 4-inch textured with a polystyrene backer strip, and 8-inch smooth with a fiberboard backer strip. Note that the overall height of the three types of siding and methods of fastening are identical. *Courtesy Crown Aluminum.*

Flat coil stock from which a multitude of shapes can be formed. *Courtesy Buy Rite Siding, Inc.*

the length of the warranty. The aluminum itself will last forever. Unlike iron or copper, which eventually oxidize (rust) all the way through, aluminum's oxide layer protects the inner metal from further corrosion.

Sizes. All siding is sold on the basis of exposure. A box marked 2 squares, for example, will cover 200 square feet of wall surface. So it makes no difference if the siding itself is a double-4 or a single-8 or what have you.

Most siding is 12½ feet long, but some companies make siding that is 13 feet long. Usually, horizontal siding is packed twenty-four panels to a box. Vertical siding is usually packed fourteen panels to a box, with one box covering 1 square.

ACCESSORIES

Most often called trim in the trade, the accessories are the pre-formed, painted metal parts that are used to hold the panels together and in place on the side of the building.

The major accessories used with all systems of siding application are:

Lineal outside and inside corners
Individual outside corners (for 8-inch panels only)
J channels
Starter strips

Then, depending on which company's products you buy, some other possibilities you may use are:

Vertical joiner strips   Drip caps
Channel runners   Barge molding
Joint molds   L channels
Backer plates   Undersill trim and more.

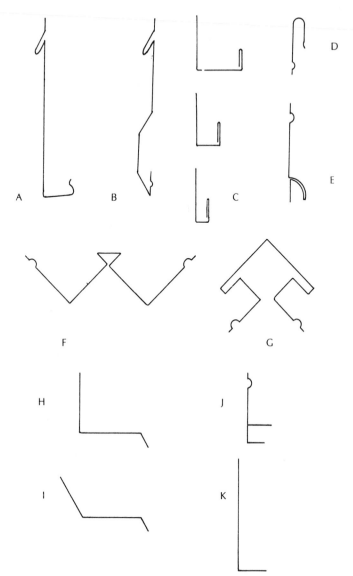

End views of the more frequently used aluminum panels and accessories (trim): (A) Horizontal panel, (B) Vertical panel, (C) J channels, (D) Utility trim, undersill trim, (E) Starter strip, (F) Inside corner, (G) Outside corner, (H) Rake edge, (I) Drip cap, (J) Fascia runner, F channel, (K) Fascia trim, L panel, fascia cap. Note that nomenclature, dimensions, and shapes vary somewhat from one manufacturer to the next.

All the accessories are available in colors and finishes that match the siding. Since the accessories are purchased separately, you don't have to use matching colors unless you want to.

SYSTEMS OF APPLICATION

Although each aluminum siding manufacturer terms his panels and accessories a special "system," they are all essentially alike. And if it appears strange that the system of applying siding is discussed prior to the actual steps necessary to apply siding, take this writer's word for it: once you understand the system, you can beat it without difficulty. (Which is true of most systems.)

The system works this way:

Each panel has two lips that act like hooks. If you look at the end of a panel, you will see them. When the panel is in place, the lower lip points inward and upward; the upper lip points outward and downward.

When you position the next-above panel, its lower lip engages the upper lip of the in-place panel. In other words, one panel hooks onto the next. But since the lowest panel is held in place (by a starter strip), you pull upward each time you install a panel. That is how the panels are locked together to make a single, continuous wall. However, the wall isn't solid. Each panel has a few tiny weep holes in its bottom edge so that moisture won't be locked behind the siding.

Where the ends of two panels meet at an outside corner, they are fitted into a lineal outside-corner accessory. This is simply a long folded strip of metal that has channels or grooves along each side that accept the panel ends. As an alternative you can join panel ends meeting at a corner with individual corner clips. However, whereas the lineal strips tend to hide imperfection, the two panels you join with a corner clip must be lined up almost perfectly.

When and where the top edge of a panel meets the underside of a window, the junction between the two can be hidden by an accessory. This may be a J channel, channel runner, or a section of undersill trim—it all depends on how you want to do the job. They all serve the same function: to hold the edge of the panel in place and to hide a raw (cut) edge.

The same is true when the siding reaches the underside of the roof extension, which is called the soffit. One or another kind of channel-type accessory is used to terminate the top edge of the panels.

Vertical panels are installed the same way. But instead of working from the bottom up, you work from one side to the other.

SOFFIT AND FASCIA

The soffit is the underside of the roof's overhang, or roof eave. (Not all homes have soffits.) The fascia is the vertical edge of the end of the roof.

Both soffit and fascia may be left as they are and painted as required. They can also be covered with metal the way the sides of the house can be covered. The same basic system is used, but it is done with metal panels made for the puropse. Soffit and fascia panels are made in a number of colors and finishes by the same companies that make aluminum siding.

TRIM TREATMENT

In this, as with the soffit and fascia, you have a choice. You can simply let the door and window frames—the house trim—be and simply paint them every four years or so. Or you can cover the trim with aluminum. Unfortunately there is no end of the number of different sizes and shapes of trim used on the doors and windows of homes under construction today or already constructed. For this reason, no manufacturer produces accessories for covering house trim. However, you can sometimes adapt the shapes they manufacture for other purposes to cover house trim.

What you cannot cover with preformed metal you can cover with metal cut and bent to shape. Again you have a choice of actions.

You can cut and bend the metal yourself, or you can hire someone to do it for you.

Cutting and bending sheet metal to fit your home's trim is not very difficult. Unfortunately, you need a metal brake, which is a large bending tool, to do this. Few tool rental shops have brakes for rent, but many of the siding suppliers do. In many instances they will let their customers use their brake as a courtesy (without charge).

3

Determining Quantity of Materials

To determine the siding quantity needed, use a steel tape, if you have one—if not, use a folding rule—and carefully measure the wall areas to be covered. Just in case you have forgotten your math, the area of a rectangle or a square is found by multiplying one side by the other. For ease of multiplication, round the fractional inches off to whole inches. The formula for the area of a triangle is height times base times ½. When you encounter a five-sided area such as the end of the house, break it down into a square or rectangle and a triangle.

Then either include the doors and windows in the overall wall area or measure the areas of the windows and doors and subtract this figure from the total—but add 10 percent to account for unavoidable waste.

Actual waste will vary with the design of the building. The more windows, doors, angles, and turns the building has, the more waste there will be. Also you waste a little more when you use both vertical and horizontal siding instead of only one type. So much for the actual siding. Now you need to measure for the accessories.

Corner posts. Measure the height of each inside and outside post, assuming that they are of different heights. You need one

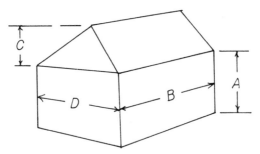

To calculate the overall area of a square or rectangular wall, multiply its height (A) by its length (B). To calculate the area of a gable end of a building, multiply its base length (D) by its height (C) by $\frac{1}{2}$.

post for each corner. If the posts available are shorter than your needs, you can overlap two lengths.

Individual outside corners. These can only be used with 8-inch horizontal siding. Measure the height of the wall. Divide by 8 inches and add 2 just to be sure. Individual corners are, of course, used in place of corner posts.

Starter strip. You need a continuous starter strip along the entire bottom edge of each wall to be sided horizontally. When the available strip isn't long enough for the wall, butt another alongside.

Channel runner, J channel, and undersill trim. These are accessories that have a cross section shaped somewhat like the letter *J*. They differ mainly in the size of the openings they have.

Channel runners are made with $\frac{1}{2}$- and $\frac{5}{8}$-inch openings. They are designed to hold the uncut side of a panel. Channel runners are used across the full width of the top of a wall sided with horizontal panels, above and below windows and doors, and for supporting one side or end of the panel or panels used for covering a soffit.

J channel, or J trim as it is often called, is made with ¾- and 1⅛-inch openings. The narrow channel is designed to accept the ends of interlocked panels without backing insultion. The wider channels are made for use with locked panels with backing insulation. These channels are used along the vertical sides of windows and doors when the wall is sided horizontally and across the top and bottom of the wall when it is sided vertically.

Undersill trim, also called utility trim, has the narrowest opening. It is used to hold the raw cut edge of a panel that has no backing insulation. It is often used across the top and bottom of windows and doors when the horizontal siding is cut lengthwise above and /or below the opening. It is sometimes used across the top of a wall when the wall is sided horizontally and the topmost panel has to be cut lengthwise.

Drip cap. Sometimes also called a rake edge or made from a metal angle designed primarily to be used as a rake edge, the drip cap is used atop all door and window frames. It is cut just as long as the width of the frame and is nailed in place atop the frame. Its purpose is to prevent water from entering behind the window or door frame. You will, however, use very little drip cap because most, if not all, the already installed wood frame windows and doors have drip caps, and most if not all new wood windows and door frames sold today come equipped with in-place drip caps.

Perforated aluminum foil. You will need as many square feet of foil as you have wall surface to cover, plus about 10 percent for overlap and unavoidable waste. Do not use anything but perforated foil. Solid foil will trap moisture and cause trouble.

Aluminum nails. Use 2-inch common aluminum nails for nailing panels having insulation backing. Use 1½-inch nails for panels without backing. About half a pound of nails per square should do it. Use painted aluminum nails 1 or 1¼ inches long for face nailing (which should be held to a minimum). Two pounds should be sufficient for the average home.

Caulking compound. Use silicone caulking only, in tube form and in colors to match your siding. The tube fits into a caulking gun. Caulking compound is more expensive in tube form, but you should not need more than one tube for the entire house. Every joint isn't caulked; only unavoidably large openings.

SOFFIT AND FASCIA

In addition to the nails and caulking you will need the following accessories for soffit and fascia.

Fascia cap. This is an L-shaped accessory that goes onto the fascia board. Select a cap that is as wide or wider than the fascia. If wider, you will have to cut it down. You need as many lineal feet of cap as you have of fascia.

Fascia runner. The total footage you require will either be equal to the total length of your soffit or twice the length of your soffit. As an alternative you can sometimes use a channel runner in place of the fascia runner.

Soffit panels. If your soffit is narrow, you may be able to use a soffit panel lengthwise. If the soffit is wider than the width of the panel, you will have to cut the panel into shorter lengths and install them crosswise. Usually this results in short pieces that cannot be used elsewhere. So measure your soffit, and if you have to cut, bear in mind the lost ends.

Double-channel runner. When you miter a corner, you need a length of the double-channel runner to make the diagonal joint.

The accessories just listed by no means exhaust the shapes available. There are more, and it is advisable that you examine all the accessories your supplier has on hand just to make certain you secure those that suit the job best, produce the least waste, and require the least cutting.

4

Installing Aluminum Soffit and Fascia

In addition to a ladder and possibly a scaffold (see Chapter 17), you may require the following tools:

Folding rule and steel tape
Spirit level
Chalk line
Razor knife
Tinsnips
Hammer
Hacksaw with a fine-tooth blade
Awl
Caulking gun
Carpenter's finishing saw (fine-tooth blade), or
    circular saw with a 10-point plywood blade
A bar of soap to lubricate the saw
Combination or steel square
Electric drill with $\frac{1}{4}$- and $\frac{1}{16}$-inch drill bits
8-inch flat-blade screwdriver.

CUTTING PANELS AND ACCESSORIES

Mark where the panel is to be cut with a square. Score the flat portion of the panel with a razor knife. Then cut the folds with the tin snips. Bend along the score until the metal breaks. You may have to open the folds a little with a screwdriver.

As an alternate you can also cut the panel with a hacksaw, but it is difficult to hold to a straight line with this saw.

The fastest, best cut in the sense of accuracy and cleanliness of edge is made with the power saw. Rent a saw table, or set up a 14-inch-wide plank on a pair of horses. Then make a simple jig

To cut aluminum
A. Mark the desired line of cut with the aid of a square.
B. Cut along the mark with a hacksaw.
C. Place the panel on a metal saw table and use a power saw. The advantages of this combination of tools are speed; clean, straight cuts; and convenience in cutting angles.
D. Or, rig up a saw table from scrap lumber as shown.
E. Or, score the metal along the line to be cut with a razor knife.
F. Then bend the metal repeatedly along the score mark until it separates.

A   B

C

D

E

F

from wood scraps to hold your saw above the panel itself. In this way, by guiding the saw along the jig you can make square cuts without scratching the surface of the panel.

To cut a panel lengthwise, score it along the mark with your razor knife. Then bend it back and forth along the line until the piece breaks free.

Accessories can be cut the same way with the same tools.

PREPARATION

The soffit is installed before the fascia, and both are most easily installed before the siding.

Start by removing the gutter from in front of the fascia. If there are galvanized drip edges, remove them too. Galvanized iron and aluminum don't mix.

Fill whatever holes are left with putty. Sandpaper or scrape the fascia and its edges free of loose paint. It is advisable to give whatever wood has been bared a coat of exterior paint at this time.

INSTALLING THE SOFFIT

Where There Is No Existing Soffit

Let us assume there is no existing soffit and that the rafters are exposed beneath the roof eaves, and further that we are dealing with a gable roof.

The first step is to carry the line formed by the bottom edge of the ends of the rafters across to the side of the building. This may be done by placing a long spirit level against the side of the building. Adjust the level until the bubble is centered. Then mark the spot where the top edge of the level touches the building. Repeat this at the other end of the roof. Now strike a line between the two marks. This can be done by driving nails partway into the wall at the two marks, stretching a chalked line tightly between the two nails, then plucking the line and letting it rebound against the wood.

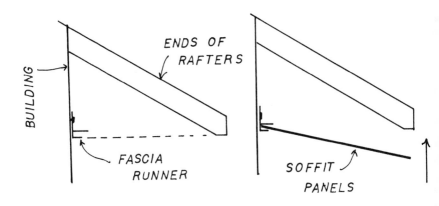

ENDS OF
RAFTERS

BUILDING

FASCIA
RUNNER

SOFFIT
PANELS

To install a soffit

A. Nail a fascia runner to the wall. Position the lower edge of the runner level with the bottom ends of the rafters.

B. Cut the soffit panels to length. Place one end of a panel into the channel. Swing the other end up against the bottom of the rafters, as shown by the arrow. Nail the panel in place.

Next, position a fascia runner with its bottom edge just on top of the chalk line you have made. Drive nails through the holes in the lip of the runner. Space the nails about 18 inches apart. The 1-inch aluminum nails will do fine.

Following that, measure and cut the soffit panels to size. If you are using them in a cross position, the correct size will be from the inside of the fascia runner to the outside edge of the fascia board less about $\frac{1}{16}$ inch. Slip the end of the cut panel into the channel, then lift the other end up against the bottom edge of the fascia board. Nail the panel to the fascia using two 1-inch nails driven gently through the provided holes.

Do not use solid panels for the entire soffit; use a number of perforated panels. You must have air circulating behind the soffit. If not, you will have moisture condensing on the panels and the wood there will rot in time.

End-of-soffit openings. Depending on the design of the building, you may have an opening at the end of the soffit at the gable side of the house. If the opening is small, you can usually seal it off with a section of panel or a section cut from flat aluminum stock. If the opening is large, it is usually best to frame it out with wood and then cover the frame with metal.

Hip roofs. These are handled a bit differently. Start by snapping a chalk line on the side of the building and installing a fascia runner as before—lip up and bottom edge on the chalk line. Cut and install soffit panels until you are within several feet of a corner. Stop and fasten a length of double-channel runner (or two lengths of J channel back to back) between the corner of the building and the corner of the roof. Resume cutting and installing panels. When you come to the double-channel runner, cut the panels at an angle to fit. Then keep on going all around the building the same way.

When There Is an Old Soffit in Place

Start by removing the molding fastened to both sides of the soffit. Then sandpaper and/or scrape off the loose paint. Nail all loose

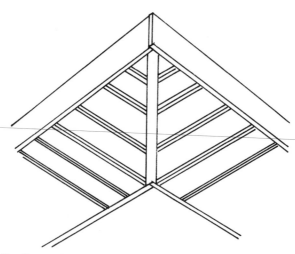

To install soffit panels around a corner, install a double channel runner between the corner of the building and the corner of the roof. Cut the panels to fit.

soffit panels or boards in place. Cut or otherwise remove any boards that project below the surface of the soffit. You want and need a smooth, flat surface to work on, or no surface at all. Remove all in-place soffit screens.

Nail a channel runner into the corner between the wall and the old soffit. The lip goes up against the soffit. Then the soffit panels are cut (as previously described), positioned, and nailed in place.

If the existing soffit has vent holes, use perforated panels beneath the vent holes. If the old soffit has no vent holes, cut some. Roughly, there should be at least 1 square foot of vent opening for every 10 lineal feet of soffit. Naturally, you position perforated panels beneath the vent holes.

If the existing soffit is beneath a hip roof, follow the previous suggestion for bringing the soffit panels around a corner.

COVERING THE FASCIA

As you know, there are fascia boards at the eaves, where the gutters are fastened. These are generally called eave fascias. And there are fascia boards at the sides of the roof's edges. These are called rake fascias.

Eave fascias. Select a fascia cap with its wide flange equal to or slightly less in width than the width of the fascia board. Press the cap up against the bottom edge of the board. Nail the vertical flange to the board using 1-inch nails of aluminum every 2 feet or so. Use the awl to start a hole for the nails.

If the cap leaves no more than ¼ inch of the fascia board exposed and the shingles overhang the fascia as they should, no more needs to be done. If there is an aluminum drip edge beneath the ends of the asphalt shingle, fine. The fascia cap goes under this. If more than ¼ inch of wood is exposed above the fascia cap, install an aluminum drip edge above the cap. (See page 140 for details on drip edge installation.)

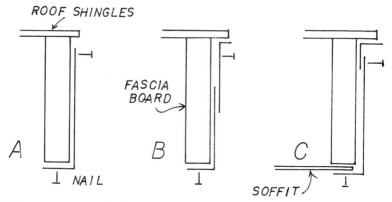

Three ways to cover a fascia:

A. Use a fascia cap wide enough to cover the entire board and nail the cap in place.

B. Use two fascia caps, one overlapping the other.

C. Use a drip cap and a wide fascia cap.

Rake fascias. The side edges of the roof are called its rakes. The procedure here depends on what you find. If there is only a rake board, install a fascia cap as suggested for the eaves. If there is an aluminum drip edge, the cap goes under the drip edge. If there is no drip edge or if the top edge of the fascia cap does not reach right up to the underside of the roof shingles, install an aluminum drip edge. Use either a roofer's aluminum drip edge or a siding corner angle.

If there is wood molding along the top edge of the rake fascia, see if you can obtain a length of aluminum trim molding to cover the wood trim. The trim-covering molding is nailed in place after you have fastened the fascia cap. If you cannot secure trim molding to fit, you can leave the wood trim uncovered and paint it if you wish, or you can remove it. In the latter case, be sure to pull all the nails, install an aluminum drip edge, and cut the roof shingles back until they overlap the roof edge by no more than ¼ inch. If you leave too much of an overhang, the wind may get beneath the sides of the shingles and pull them off. But do not cut yet if you

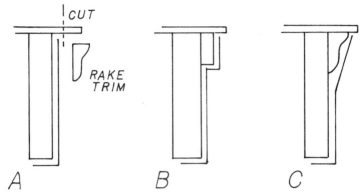

Three ways to cover a rake fascia:

A. Remove the rake trim (molding) and use a fascia cap of the proper width.

B. Replace the rake trim with a rectangular strip of wood and cover that and the rake as shown.

C. Find or bend trim to fit over the rake trim molding and the rake board. Use utility trim to hold top edge of metal in place if necessary.

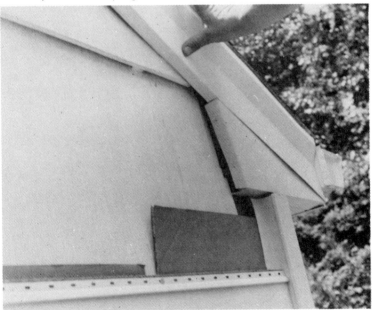

Rake trim made from sheet stock bent to shape.

Short soffit panels applied to rake-end soffit. Top edge of rake fascia trim held in place by utility trim. *Courtesy Buy Rite Siding, Inc.*

Nailing soffit panels in place. *Courtesy Aluminum Association.*

Completed eave soffit, same building. *Courtesy Aluminum Association.*

Building overhang treated like a soffit.
Panels installed lengthwise.

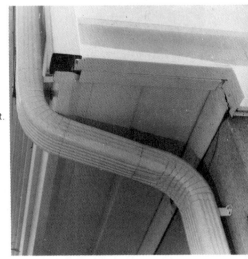

A

Covering a porch ceiling with soffit panels.
  A. J channel nailed above door frame.
  B. Panel ends slipped into J channel. Other ends nailed to roof frame.
  C. Completed ceiling.

B

C

expect to build out the wall and so have to extend the fascia as well (see Chapter 6).

Join cap and rake trim sections by simply overlapping them a few inches. To bring a cap around a corner, cut a 45-degree piece out of the narrow flange at the corner; then just pull the metal around. If a lump develops, place a board on top of the high spot and strike the board lightly with a hammer. Never strike the metal directly; you will mark it.

There is no need for a complex joint or overlap where the rake cap meets the eave cap. Just let the ends of the metal strips butt each other and use a little caulking to seal the joint.

One final point: Always keep your hands clean when working on the soffit (and siding, too). If you don't, you may end up spending considerable time washing your fingerprints off.

5

Covering the House Trim

At this point you have either covered the soffit and fascia or you have decided to let them be and just paint them when necessary. You are now ready to begin work covering the house trim, assuming you are not merely going to paint it.

TOOLS

In addition to the tools listed in the previous chapter, you will need a crosscut wood saw and the use of a metal brake.

WINDOW AND DOOR FRAME BUILDUP

Whether or not you cover the house trim, if you are going to side the building with any formed strip siding, you have to make the following test and decision:

Take a convenient piece of J channel that has the correct opening for the panels you are going to use and place it in position against the building (or atop whatever furring material you plan to use to build the wall out) alongside a window or door frame. This is how the channel will look when it is later installed. If the front surface of the channel is flush or below the surface of the

Your first step preparatory to covering the house trim and applying siding is to remove all the shutters, gutters, and the like from the exterior of the house. In-window air-conditioners can be left in place. Whether or not you remove the storm windows depends on whether or not you anticipate needing to replace the storm windows in the future.

Whether or not you are going to cover the house trim, all window and door sills must be cut flush with the sides of their frames.

frame, no problem. If the channel projects beyond, you have to decide if it projects an objectionable distance. On some homes and in the eyes of some individuals, anything up to an inch is acceptable. To others, anything beyond a half inch is intolerable.

If you fall into the latter group and you want to correct the projection, the solution lies in simply building the frames out. This is done by nailing strips of wood atop the frame. Make the strips out of 1-inch-thick number-2 pine just as wide as the frame pieces. Face-nail the strips in place, using no more than two or three nails per strip. Countersink the nailheads. Apply strips to the top and side portions of all the windows and doors. There is no need to do anything with the sills.

This done, take a small saw and cut the protruding ends of all the sills—in door frames and window frames—flush with the sides of their frames. *This has to be done whether or not you cover the frames.*

Incidentally, if you are not going to cover the frames, be certain to give all the knots in the wood a coat of shellac before you paint.

MEASURING THE FRAMES

Examine the window and door frames. If you have the old-type storm windows and storm doors that rest on the outer surfaces of the frames, you do not need more than a simple angle of aluminum to cover these frame members. In such cases the best job is obtained by removing the storms, applying the aluminum, and then replacing the storms.

If the storm windows and storm doors do not rest on the front surfaces of the frames but rest inside, all you need to cover the sides of the frames is a simple U-shaped channel. If there are no storm windows, you will need a U-shaped channel with a second fold alongside.

The tops of the window and door frames require a simple angle. The sills require a channel.

To decide whether or not you want to build the house trim out, place a section of the J channel you plan to use alongside a door or window frame, as shown. This will give you a preview of what the job will look like. NOTE: If you plan to build the wall out with either foamed sheet, plywood, or furring strips or straps, you must place whichever you use behind the J channel to get a true preview of what the job will look like.

The strips of wood you nail to the sides of the window and door frames must be of exactly the same width as the frame they cover. There is usually no need to build out the sills or the top of the frames.

In any case, measure the sills, side pieces, and top sections of the window and door frames very carefully. Sketch the cross section of each piece and add the dimensions to the drawing. Then multiply the length of the various pieces by the number of pieces required, to find the total length of the various folded aluminum shapes you will need to cover the house trim.

SHAPING THE TRIM COVERING

Trim covering is usually made from 0.019-inch-thick aluminum that you can purchase in strip form from the same company that supplies the aluminum siding. It can be had bare or painted in any of several colors. Never use the bare. It will not look "right" with painted siding.

From here on, you have two choices: you can bend the strip yourself or hire someone to bend it into shape for you.

To bend or form the metal yourself, you require a metal brake, which is a bending machine. The machine is too expensive to purchase for a single job, but some of the larger tool rental shops may have it, or your supplier may let you use his.

To use the brake place the strip of aluminum sideways in the machine and lock it in place with the vise. Then pull the brake handle up and release it. That makes a single bend. Then release the strip, move it sideways the required distance, and bend again—and so on. There really isn't very much to it except learning just how much extra metal you must allow for the bend itself. For example, to make a channel with an inside opening of 1 inch by 1 inch, you have to allow about $\frac{1}{16}$ inch for the corners. This varies with the thickness of the metal and the sharpness and angle of the bends. But it is not too difficult, and you can soon learn just by practice.

If you are going to hire someone to do the bending for you, your best bet is a local tinsmith. (A siding applicator may be a bit peeved at you for doing your own siding and may charge more than the tinsmith.) In any case, bring the sketches to the smith and

Using a brake.

A. The metal to be bent is slid beneath the locking bar. The lever (under hand) is raised, clamping the metal firmly in place.

B. The lower half of the brake is raised, bending the metal to the desired angle. This brake is 12 feet long and can bend strips of metal of an equal or lesser length to angles as small as 45 degrees. *Courtesy Buy Rite Siding, Inc.*

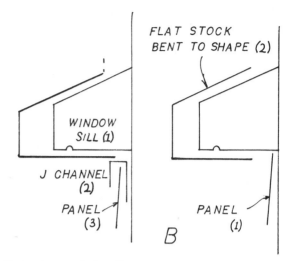

Two ways to cover a door or window sill.

A. Cover the sill (1) first. Install the J channel or utility trim (2), and then apply the panel (3).

B. A new method, saving material and time but requiring a more exact fitting of parts. The siding (1) is installed first, with care taken to bring the siding's top edge up against the underside of the sill. Then the sill covering (2) is applied.

Covering the sill first. Here the sheet stock has been cut and bent to fit the sill of three side-by-side windows. *Courtesy Buy Rite Siding, Inc.*

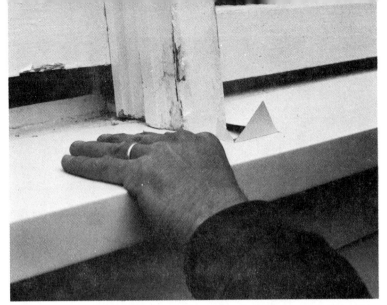

Close-up. Note vertical tabs. These will go beneath the bent metal that will be placed over the vertical portion of the frame. Tabs make for a better appearing job and help keep water from running behind the sill covering, but tabs are not absolutely necessary. *Courtesy Buy Rite Siding, Inc.*

Completed window sill done in the three-step method shown in A, in the drawing on page 50. Note how the top edge of the panel fits behind the J channel or utility trim.

Sill completed using the two-step method shown in B in the drawing on page 50. Note how top edge of panel is positioned behind bent metal that covers the sill. (Opening helps drain sill of moisture and should not be caulked.)

Two ways to cover the top of a window or door frame:

A. When the wall and trim are not furred out and the original frame and cap project beyond the completed wall (or will project when completed), the aluminum angle is positioned as shown. The drip cap is left in place.

B. When the wall and trim are furred out, a wide metal angle is used which goes up well beyond the top of the frame. Then the J channel used to hold the ends of the panels is carried across the top of the window. A length of utility trim is positioned on top of it. Finally, the wall panels are installed.

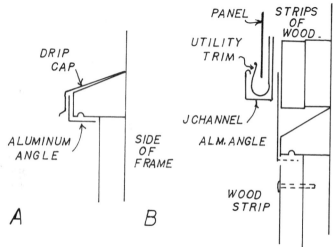

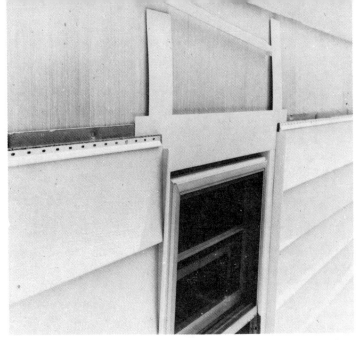

Partially completed window frame. Note how the vertical J channels have been brought up past the frame. Note the wide metal angle at the top of the window reaching above the top edges of the in-place panels. The metal strip hanging at an angle above has been nailed there temporarily. It will be used for the sill. The two flat strips rising above the window are the ends of the metal trim used to cover the sides of the window. It was easier not to cut the metal to size.

End view of the same window upon completion. Note the way the J channel has been positioned horizontally. Note the utility trim holding the cut edge of the panel in place. (You can also use the lower edge of a panel here if you wish.) Note that the opening (A) has not been sealed with caulking cement. This, like the openings at the bottom of the window frame, must be left open for drainage.

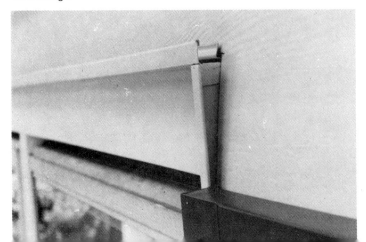

Front view of the same portion of the window frame. The top of the window frame is completely hidden by the metal.

Covering the sides of a window frame. *Courtesy Buy Rite Siding, Inc.*

To cover a fixed window, the aluminum is bent to shape and nailed over the frame and mullions. Just a few small nails are necessary. *Courtesy Buy Rite Siding, Inc.*

have him make a few sample pieces first. Try these for size, and if they are satisfactory, have him bend up strips just as long as his brake, which may be 10 to 20 feet long. There is no point in having him make a lot of short pieces when you can cut the long strip into pieces yourself.

APPLYING THE HOUSE TRIM COVERING

The sill. Use a piece of aluminum several inches longer than the sill. Fold the metal to fit over the sill. Carefully measure and cut rectangular indentations on one edge of the sill cover so that it can be slipped between the vertical portions of the frame. You want a close fit here. Slit the ends of the metal and bend the ends back over the ends of the sill. Trim the excess metal. Use an awl to start a few holes for nails. Use just a few 1-inch aluminum nails to hold the sill cover in place. Position the nails out of sight if possible.

The sides. Cut the side trim covers from pieces of metal 1 inch longer than the height of the frame sides. Bend the metal to fit. Cut back the upper edges, leaving a projecting tab. Place the folded metal over the wood trim, the tab on the top of the cover projecting onto the top of the frame. Again, use just a few nails to hold this trim cover in place.

The top. Cut a piece of strip aluminum as long as the upper horizontal portion of the frame. Bend it to fit. This cover goes on top of the aforementioned tabs and under the aluminum drip cap. Nail in place.

FINISHING UP

Use just enough silicone caulking of a matching color to close any openings that may be unsightly. Use as little as possible, since caulking changes color with time and collects dirt. Openings that will drain by themselves do not have to be sealed.

6

Applying Horizontal Aluminum Siding

At this point you have finished with the soffit, fascia, and house trim one way or another. You have tested the siding J channels against the house trim and have either accepted the resulting appearance or have built out the house trim.

You have measured up your building and know how much siding, nails, perforated aluminum foil, type and quantity of accessories, and other material you will need. You have also decided on the type, color, and design of your siding and its insulation. In a word, you are about ready to apply the siding.

This chapter covers the application of horizontal siding. The following chapter covers the application of vertical siding. If you are only going to apply horizontal siding, you need only read this chapter. But if you are going to apply both types of siding or only vertical siding, you have to read both chapters.

PREPARING THE BUILDING

Start by carefully examining the building. Stand at each corner and look along each side. See if there are any hollows or bulges in the walls. If you are not certain, work with a friend and stretch a line (string) from corner to corner and visually check the distance from the string to the side of the building, while both of you lift the string upward.

Hollows or bulges of less than 1 inch in 20 feet of wall length can be ignored. When the wall's wandering is greater than this—when you see the fault immediately—it has to be corrected. You cannot hide a deformity in the wall by siding over it.

Correcting a hollow. Hollows are more easily corrected than bulges. The method is simply to build the wall out over the low area. This may be done with furring strips, which are lengths of 1- by 2-inch or 1- by 3-inch wood nailed vertically onto the side of the building. It can also be done with straps, which are similar pieces of wood nailed horizontally across the side of the building.

Furring strips are generally used when the old siding is vertical. Straps are generally used when the old siding is horizontal.

Before you nail the strips permanently in place, nail them temporarily and check their surface against the balance of the wall with the line, as previously suggested. If necessary, shim the low spots out with pieces of wood. Cut the high areas back by planing the wood down as needed. If too much planing is required, use thinner strips of wood.

When you do nail the strips permanently in place, use 8-penny common nails. Position the furring strips or straps so that they will be beneath the nailing holes in the siding. Otherwise you will have trouble nailing the siding on in those areas. And try to get at least a few of the strip and/or strap nails into the studs. You can locate the studs very often by locating the nails in the old siding. When you see a row of nailheads one above another, that is where the stud is.

Correcting a bulge. This is more difficult, since you must actually remove some of the old siding. If it is just a board or two that needs cutting back, little trouble. Remember, you are going to install new siding, so even if you have to remove a portion of the old siding, no harm is done. However, if there are a lot of bulges and they are quite prominent, consider building out the low areas around them by strapping or furring out the entire rest of the wall.

But remember, when you build out a wall, you usually have to bring the fascia out an equal distance. This can be done easily by nailing a second fascia atop the old if there is no problem with the roof shingles. If the shingles will be short and it is very important the wall be brought out, use an aluminum drip edge under the shingle ends. (See the chapters on roofing in the latter part of this book.)

After you are finished with the hollows and bulges, go over the entire surface of the building and look for loose siding, popped nails, and the like. Drive all nails home. Make certain the house trim, corner boards, etc., are tight. If you haven't removed the leaders and their supporting hardware, do so now. Remove the shutters, mailbox, flower boxes, etc. You want a firm, projection-free wall surface so that you can apply the siding without problems.

SIDING OVER BRICK AND STUCCO

Simply install furring strips atop the old wall. Space the strips 16 inches apart on center so that the strips lie beneath the nailing holes in the siding. Position additional strips so there is one strip adjacent to both sides of all window and door frames. Fasten straps beneath and above the frames.

Obviously, when you bring the wall out by strapping and furring, you have to bring the window and door frames out an equal distance and perhaps more. To check this, place a J channel atop the furring strip adjacent to the side of the window. Then use your judgment as to whether or not you want to build the frames out.

CHECK FOR SQUARENESS

One naturally assumes that any structure as large and as expensive as a building has square sides, that at least the roof line is

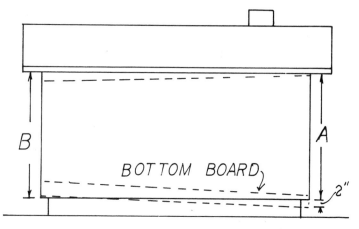

If end A of the building is, say, 2 inches shorter than end B, you have the choice of either adding a bottom board, as shown, to make both ends equal, or you can cut the topmost siding panel at an angle, as shown.

parallel to the bottom edge of the wall. Unfortunately, this is not so in a sufficient number of instances to make this next step almost mandatory if you want a good-looking job.

You have to measure. A simple visual inspection won't tell you what you need to know. To do this properly, it is best to use a steel tape.

Start at any corner of the house and measure from the soffit or the rake to the bottom of the building at that point. The best and most accurate way is to drive a nail partway into the building at the top of the wall, hang a tape on the nail, and measure away. Record the height of the first corner you measure on the bottom of the wall nearby. Then go to the second corner, measure away, and record the height on the wall. Measure every inside and outside corner of the building and carefully write the results down.

When the corners are of different heights, the short ones must be extended to match the long ones. If you do not do this but simply start the first and bottom panel flush with the bottom of the building or prefectly level, you will end up cutting the last and top siding panel lengthwise at a diagonal. And this angularly cut panel will be obvious when you look at the side of the building.

It is not necessary that the panels be positioned perfectly horizontal. In fact, if you install the panels perfectly horizontal and the building is actually tilted, the finished work will look horrible. Every window and every door will be obviously tilted. When the entire house tilts—windows, doors, and panels—the eye accepts it all as being perfectly level and orthogonal. But when there is a slight difference in angle between the panels and the frames and ends of the building, the tilt is magnified visually. The entire house looks like it is going to fall down.

Note that the above is contrary to what you will read in most if not all the instruction pamphlets provided by some of the manufacturers and the Aluminum Association. But it is the way the experts do it.

PROVIDE A FLAT SUPPORTING SURFACE

When you apply panels, with or without insulation, over clapboard with 4 or 6 inches of exposure, the panels hang flat without any problem. When you attempt to apply the same 8-inch-wide panels over shingles and shakes with 14 or more inches of exposure and "shadow lines" 1 inch deep, the panels follow the tilt of the shakes.

In such cases you must provide a flat supporting surface. This can be done in any of three ways. You can nail furring strips, consisting of wood lath, to the wall. The lath is positioned vertically and spaced about 16 inches apart. You can use the same lath as straps, meaning horizontal furring strips. The difference is that the wall is not built out as far. And you can use the new, foamed sheathing board.

Called core board by the trade, it consists of two heavy sheets of brown paper with a ¼-inch layer of styrofoam between. Core board can be cut with a razor knife, held in place with a few nails, and trimmed to size after it is on the wall. There is little measuring; it is simply nailed over the entire wall. Since it has an R factor of about 1.6 it adds considerably to the siding's overall insulating

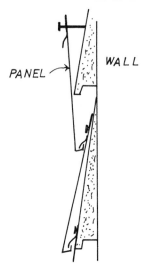

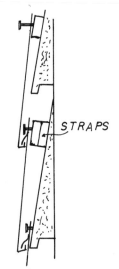

Why it is necessary to provide a flat supporting surface when the width of the panel is less than the width or exposure of the old, in-place siding.

How straps of wood lath can be used to provide a flat supporting surface.

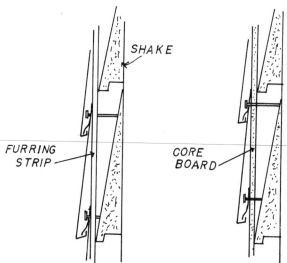

How wood lath can be used as furring strips for the same purpose.

How core board can be used to provide insulation plus a flat supporting surface. Remember, the nails are not driven home, so there is no need for support strength.

properties. Generally, aluminum foil is not used with core board. It isn't necessary.

In most instances, when you fur, strap, or cover the wall with core board it is necessary to build the house trim—corners, bottom, and top edge trim—out an equal distance. The easy way to check this is to build out the wall first and then see how the surface that will carry the panels relates to the balance of the building.

INSTALLING STARTER STRIPS AND CORNERS

Need for bottom boards. For best appearance it is advisable to bring out the bottom edge of the wall to be sided by a distance equal to the thickness of the backer board or other insulation that may be used with the siding. Generally a strip of plywood about ¼ inch thick and 6 inches wide satisfies this requirement. If you do not use this bottom board spacer, the first siding panel will be that much closer to the wall than the following panels. The starter strips are nailed to this board—but do not do any cutting and nailing yet. You have to check your corner heights first.

If all the corners are the same height, the bottom board goes flush with the bottom edge of the wall. If you are going to use individual corners, the board ends reach to the outside corners, but their ends do not overlap. If you are going to use lineal posts on the outside corners, cut the bottom boards short of the corners by 2¾ inches. No matter what is done to the boards at the outside corners, they are always cut short of the inside corners by the same 2¾ inches. Nail the bottom boards in place using 8-penny common nails every 12 inches or so.

If all the corners are not the same height and you are going to use a bottom board exactly 6 inches wide, go to the longest corner. Measure 6 inches up and drive a nail partway into the building at this point. Go to the short corner. Measure up and make a mark at a distance of exactly 6 inches. Read your notations. If, for example, they read, this corner short by 2 inches, measure down 2 inches from the mark you just made on the side of the building. Drive a nail partway into the building at the second mark. Now snap a chalk line between the two nails.

Next, pull out the nails and place your bottom board's top edge against the building and flush with the chalk line. Nail the board in place. When you're finished, you have a rectangular or square building side with both vertical edges exactly equal in height. The bottom edge, however, may or may not be level.

Installing the starter strip. The starter strip is now nailed in place atop the bottom board. The lip edge of the starter strips goes out and down. The starter strip or strips start and end about ¼ inch short of the ends of the bottom board. If there is no bottom board and you are using lineal outside corners, the starter strips begin 3 inches short of the outside corners. If you are using individual outside corners, the starter strip should be positioned 1 inch shy of the corner.

In all cases the starter strip is cut 3 inches short of an inside corner, and the bottom edge of the starter strip is always flush with the bottom edge of the bottom board.

Join starter strip ends by simply butting them together, but take care to see that they are aligned. Use 2-inch aluminum nails every 16 inches or so. Incidentally, you don't have to install all the bottom boards, if used, and all the starter strips on all the walls at this time. You can install the boards and strips on one wall at a time if you wish. With one exception: If you are going to use individual corner pieces, work on both sides of the corner at the same time. It is easier to keep the panels aligned if you do.

Applying the foil. Although you can apply the foil first and then the furring and strapping and bottom boards if you wish, it is generally easier to install the perforated foil afterward. Little or nothing in insulation is lost if you cut the foil and overlap ends or if you lay the foil right over the furring strips. If there is no wind, use a few roofing nails to hold the sheet in place. If there is a wind,

Two wood laths, one atop the other, have been used as a spacer beneath the starting strip. The bottom of the lath furring strip is brought out with a wood spacer to bring the lath's surface nearly flush with the starting strip.

Side view of the same job. Note the spaces between the lath furring strips and shakes on the wall of the building.

Another view of the same job. Furring-strip ends have been positioned alongside one another.

Nailing the panels in place.

A J channel has been positioned alongside the door frame. Another has been positioned atop the concrete slab.

This is how the panel will be fitted atop the concrete porch and against the side of the door.

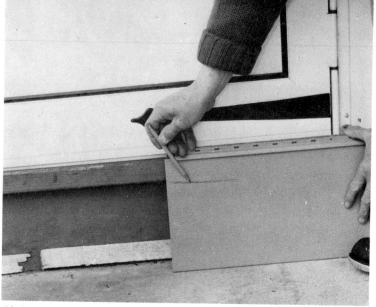

Marking a panel preliminary to cutting it to fit beneath the door sill. The top edge (nailing flange) is discarded.

use a small staple gun—the kind that is used in an office—to fasten the foil to the wall. You can also use a large heavier stapling gun, which can be rented from a tool-rental house.

Fastening the lineal corner posts in place. Examine a post. See that it has not been bent and that its flanges have not been spread. Hold the post against the corner of the house. See if it rests smoothly against the house trim. If not, find out what is wrong. The post may be bent or the corner trim may be loose or damaged. Correct as necessary.

When the post can be fitted smoothly over the corner, adjust and position it so that its bottom end extends about ¼ inch below the edge of the nearby starter strip. Drill a ¼-inch hole 2 inches down from the top of one flange and more or less centered in the width of the flange. Drive a 1¼-inch aluminum nail through this hole. Make the nail snug, but *do not drive it home.* With the single nail holding the corner in place you can now drive 1- or 1¼-inch nails through the provided nail slots, taking care to position the nails in the center of the slot and not to crimp the metal. The metal must be free to move a little beneath the nails.

Go to the other corner and repeat the procedure: Hang the post from a single nail then drive the balance of the nails through the center of the slots. The purpose of all this is to allow the metal to expand downward when its temperature increases.

If a single post will not reach the top of the wall, install a second post. You start at the bottom of the wall with the first piece and use the same nailing technique. Then install the upper post or post section. An overlap of an inch or so is plenty. Keep the top of the post about ¼ inch clear of the soffit or rake.

INSTALLING PANELS BETWEEN CORNER POSTS

For the sake of ease of discussion, let us assume that you are going to work on a side wall of the building that has no windows or doors. Such a wall is also a good place actually to start because it is the easiest to side.

Measuring the panels. Pick up the first panel. Remember, if your hands are not clean you may be spending hours later removing fingerprints. Hold the panel paint side out, nailing edge (the edge with the long holes) up, and slide the end of the panel carefully into the channel in a corner post. Let the panel move down and rest on the starter strip. Swing the panel against the building and the second corner post (assuming one panel is long enough to reach from one corner to the next). Make certain the panel is horizontal. Then use a grease pencil and make a mark on the panel ⅛ inch short of where you estimate the inside edge of the corner post's channel to be. Remove the panel and cut it on the mark, as previously described. If the panel is insulated, you will have to remove a 2-inch-wide band to facilitate cutting and to enable this panel and the above panel to fit into the corner post channels. If you have measured accurately, your cut panel will be ⅛ inch shorter than the distance from the inside of one channel to the other. In other words, the panel will be shorter than the provided space by ⅛ inch. (A little more will do no harm.)

Installing the panels. Hold the panel in a horizontal position below the wall. Lift the panel and guide its ends into the post channels. Slowly and carefully push the bottom of the panel up against the starter strip lip and continue pushing until the panel has fully engaged the lip. If the insulation is not glued to the back of the panel, the insulation is dropped into place at this time. Now you nail the panel in place.

This is easy but requires care. Don't get carried away. Use 2-inch aluminum nails (1½-inch when no insulation is used). Drive the nails through the provided holes, positioning the nails midway in the long holes. Use one nail every 16 inches and try to locate the studs. You can tell by the way the nail responds when you hit it.

Now comes the hardest part: restraint. Do not even think about driving the nails home. Their heads must stand clear of the metal by at least 1/32 inch. In other words the panels hang on the nails. *The panels are not nailed to the wall.* If you nail the panels to the wall, you will bend the panels, lock them to the wall, make the finished job look bad, and cause the panels to squeak with weather changes.

The following panel is cut to the same length as the first. To install the following panel, slip its end partially under the end of the in-place panel and partially into the channel. Then move it farther into the channel while you simultaneously lift the panel into place. Pull upward to make certain the interlock—the folded hook on the bottom of the panel—has fully engaged the lower panel. Then nail as previously described.

Continue to cut and install panels until you reach the top of the wall or near its top. Then hold off until this portion of the job is discussed a little farther on.

Steps in applying aluminum siding atop core board:

A. Core board is nailed to the wall of the building, in this case, the side of a screened porch. Small spaces are intentionally left between board ends to permit moisture to pass through.

B. The core board is nailed over a corner.

C

C. A corner post is nailed on top of the core board.
D. A strip of lath is nailed to the bottom edge of the wall to bring it out.
E. Core board is nailed over the wall and the strip of lath. Just a few nails are required.
F. The starter strip is nailed along the bottom edge of the wall. The end of the strip is short of the corner post.

D

E

F

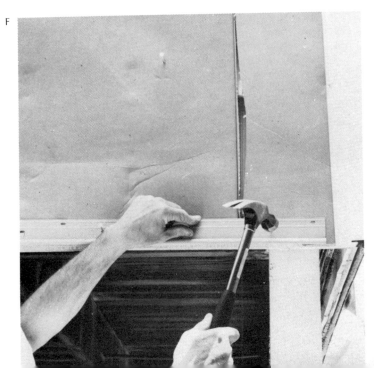

G

G. The end of the first panel is slipped into place. It must be shy of the inside, vertical surface of the corner post by 1/16 inch.

H. One or two nails are partially driven through the panel holes and into the wall. Then the strip of insulation is dropped in place behind the panel.

I. Now the panel is nailed to the wall. Note the space between the nail head and the panel. Note that the insulation is beneath the nailing holes. If the insulation is too narrow to reach this high by itself, it must be lifted up before nailing.

J. The first panel has been nailed in place. Now the following panel is positioned, the insulation dropped in, and the panel is pulled up against the "hook" on the in-place panel and nailed. And so it goes for the balance of the wall. *Courtesy Buy Rite Siding, Inc.*

H

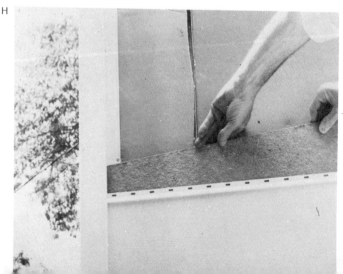

Joining panel ends. To this point we have assumed that one panel will be long enough or longer than necessary to reach from one corner of the building to the next. When this is not the case the panel ends have to be joined.

The ends of the double-4 panels are joined by simply sliding the cut end beneath the uncut end for a distance of at least ½ inch. More will do no harm, if the insulation is cut out of the way.

The 8-inch panels are sometimes handled differently. Luxaclad —and possibly other companies—makes a metal clip into which the ends of the flat 8-inch panels are slipped after interfering insulation is removed. All the other companies make a backer strip for use behind the 8-inch panel-end joints. Most experienced siding applicators do not use this strip, because it swells with time and causes the joint to bulge outward. Experienced applicators handle the 8-inch panels just like the double-4s. What insulation is present is cut back enough to allow the end of one panel to be pushed inside the other.

Properly overlapped panel ends. The flat portions of the panels are atop one another. The nailing edge or hook edge of one has been cut back 1/2 inch or more.

Look down the length of each panel as you apply it. Minor bulges and hollows can be corrected by loosening or tightening the supporting nails a little bit.

When making any of these joints, you will find it easier if you just use a few partially driven-in nails on the in-place panel. Doing so will allow you to move the panel a bit while you maneuver the second panel into place.

The rule to bear in mind while doing all this is that it is best to make the joint laps face away from traffic. This means simply that the cut edge should be hidden beneath the uncut edge and that the latter edge should point in a direction away from the usual flow of traffic. For example, if you are paneling the side of the house, install the uncut length of panel near the front of the house. Install the cut portion of panel to rear side of the house. Let the uncut panel overlap the cut end. In this way, the cut and unpainted end is invisible, and the visible end cannot easily be seen from the front of the building, where there is the most traffic.

A

Steps in applying panels to the side of a dormer.
A. A lineal corner has been fastened to one corner of the dormer. A J channel has been fastened to the top and bottom of the dormer's sides. Here the first panel is being fitted into place.
B. The end of the panel that meets both the roof of the building and the eave of the dormer has been cut to the necessary angle, as has the backer board. Both are being fitted into place.
C. Measuring the space the uppermost panel will cover.
D. Nailing the last panel in place. *Courtesy Aluminum Association.*

B

C

D

An air-conditioner opening can be trimmed out much like a window.

Staggering the joints. Select or cut the panels so that one joint is not directly above another. If the joints are in a vertical line, the siding is weakened somewhat. Also, if the joints are less than 6 inches apart, they may leak. For best results and appearance try to keep the joints several feet apart.

INSTALLING INDIVIDUAL OUTSIDE CORNERS

Install one starter strip 1 inch shy of the corner. Go around the corner and install a second starter strip 1 inch short of the same corner. Make certain the ends of both strips are perfectly level, even if you have to cheat a bit and raise or lower one strip end a fraction of an inch.

Install one panel, taking care to hold its end ¾ inch short of the corner of the house. Make certain the interlock is fully engaged. Do the same with a second panel, around the corner. Place a spirit level on the bottom edges of the two ends of the panels meeting at the corner. If the panel ends are level, fine; keep on going. If not, correct before going any farther. The individual corners will not fit correctly if the panel ends are not perfectly level with one another.

Next you can install the corners. There are several kinds. One type is simply pushed into place. The type made by Luxaclad, for example, is held in place by two aluminum nails. Again, these nails are never driven home. They are always left protruding about $\frac{1}{32}$ inch clear of the metal.

No matter what type of corner piece you install, always make certain that pieces are pushed all the way up. If you can't get a neat joint at the corner, check for a bent interlock or for a panel that has not engaged its interlock fully. Somehow the panel ends have gotten out of alignment. You just have to find where and correct the trouble.

WORKING WITH WINDOWS AND DOORS

Windows and doors are treated similarly. Since you will encounter their sills first, they are discussed next.

Sill treatment. The method described following will probably differ from the method you will use when you gain a little experience, but it is almost foolproof and easier to explain. So here goes.

Side until a sill—of a doorway or window—prevents you from applying one full-width panel. When this occurs, place the panel beneath the sill in the position you want the panel to occupy. Do not forget to account for any necessary overlap. With a grease pencil mark the width of the sill on the panel. Then place the panel alongside the sill, taking care to see that the interlock—the panel's

Use a J channel when you need to terminate the panels anyplace other than an outside corner.

lower lip—is properly engaged. Now mark the depth of the sill on the panel. Remove the panel and draw the outline of the area that is to be removed. Use snips to cut across the panel and the razor knife to make the lengthwise cut. Remove the backing if any. Slowly bend the cut portion back and forth until it breaks off.

Return to the wall and try the panel in place. Note the space behind the cut portion of the panel, directly beneath the sill. Measure its depth. Remove the panel. Find a length of wood just as thick or a fraction less thick than the depth of the space behind the panel. Cut the wood. (Make it as long as the sill.) Nail the strip of wood beneath the sill. Cut a ½- or ⅝-inch channel runner to a length equal to the width of the sill. Nail the channel runner to the wood beneath the sill; the channel opening facing down. Slip the panel into place. The cut edge should enter the channel runner. If the channel runner doesn't provide a sufficiently tight fit, use a length of undersill trim. Face nails will not be seen here, but they will buckle the metal visibly.

Side frame treatment. Cut J channel stock into lengths equal to the height of the window and door frames. Since the panel directly beneath the sill is already in place, you will have to slide the J channel down behind it. Do this, keeping the large flange of the J channel against the building wall and the bottom of its channel against the window or door frame. The top of the J channel should terminate flush with the top of the frame. Start a few holes in the channel flange with an awl, and nail it in place with 1¼-inch aluminum nails. One nail every 2 feet is plenty.

Now you can continue applying panels as before. Instead of both ends of the panel or panels terminating in corner posts, one or both ends of the panels terminate in J channels.

Paneling above the frame. The problem you may encounter will be the reverse of the problem you met beneath the sill. As before, hold the panel in place to measure the width of the cut, this time to be taken out of the bottom edge of the panel. Then measure its depth and cut the panel. If while cutting you happen to crimp the interlock, open it up again with a screwdriver.

Next, select a J channel with a width or opening suited to the cut edge of the panel. Cut the J channel just as long as the width of the frame. Temporarily position the cut panel and see whether or not the J channel needs to be furred out. Fur or not as required. Nail the J channel in place, nailing flange up. Then install the cut panel and you are ready to continue.

If there is no drip cap above the frame, you should install one before the J channel is nailed in place atop the frame.

INSTALLING THE TOPMOST PANEL

If your topmost panel just fits, fine. But as is more likely, the last panel will be too wide for the space, in which case you will have to cut it lengthwise. First, of course, you will have to determine where to cut.

If you still have to install a soffit, leave 1 inch of space above the topmost edge of the panel. If no work is to be done to the soffit, leave ¼ inch of clearance above the top of the panel. Next, take a short piece of panel scrap. Estimate how much has to be cut from the top panel to make it fit, then cut this much from the scrap. Try it in place. When you have finished testing the cut scrap, you can safely cut the last panel. Remove the insulation, score the line for the cut with a razor knife, and bend along the line until the metal parts.

Hold the panel in place. Note its top edge. Depending on the nature of the building siding and whether or not the panel is insulated, the top edge of the panel may be inward of the other panels. Hold the panel away from the building and measure the distance needed to correct this condition. If needed, nail a wood strap across the side of the building. Use wood having a thickness equal to or a little less than the spacing needed.

Next, nail ½-inch or ⅝-inch channel runner or even sill trim atop the strap—whichever provides the tightest fit. Slip the last panel up into place. If you are certain the interlock has taken hold and the panel still doesn't feel secure, lock it in place using ½-inch self-tapping stainless steel screws driven up through the weep holes. One every second or third hole is sufficient.

WORKING UNDER A GABLE END

The only difference between applying horizontal siding beneath the gable end of a building and beneath an eave side is that beneath the gable you are working on a wall that has a triangular shape. This simply means you must cut the panels where they meet the angle of the roof at a similar angle.

Start by installing a J channel with a suitable opening beneath the roof soffit or beneath the fascia rake boards. Temporarily hold one length of panel in place and slide it sideways until it touches the J channel. Have someone hold the panel for you. Place a straight-sided board across the end of the panel and against the soffit. With a grease pencil draw a line across the panel along the edge of the board. Remove the board and the panel. You now have the angle at which you must cut the end of the panel. Cut the panel and save the scrap piece. That will serve as your guide for cutting the other panels.

Install the panels as before, sliding the cut ends of the panels into the J channel. Again, watch the way the panel ends run so that you do not fail to stagger the joints.

When you get to the top, you may find that the last panel just makes it, which is fine. If, on the other hand, you find you are left with an open triangle just a few inches across, a space too small for a piece of panel, cover the space with metal. Use a section of similiarly colored metal taken either from a piece of scrap panel or from some of the sheet strip used for covering the house trim. With your tin snips cut a triangle to cover the opening at the underpeak of the roof. Drill a few holes through it and fasten it in place atop the J trim and siding panel.

7

Applying Vertical Aluminum Siding

The difference between applying horizontal paneling and vertical paneling lies mainly in the way the vertical panels are started and terminated. The balance of the work is almost the same. The panels lock onto one another to form a continuous metallic wall by means of their interlocks, just the way the horizontal panels do. And the panels are fastened to the wall by nailing, just as are the horizontal panels.

PREPARING THE BUILDING

Prepare the building as previously suggested. Remove all projecting boards, drive all loose nails home, fasten all loose boards or remove them. Then check the walls for bulges and depressions and hollows and correct them, as previously suggested, if necessary.

To determine how your window and door frames will look when the building is sided, place ½- or ⅝-inch channel runners or J channels along the sides of the frames. Use whatever size will provide the better fit with the *sides* of the panels you are going to use. Then hold a length of either ¾- or 1⅛-inch J channel beneath the door and window sills to see how the job is going to look there. In this way you will be able to visualize the finished appearance of the wall quickly and you can then decide if and how much you want to build the house trim out.

Remember, if you are going to cover the house trim with metal, that is the next step.

If the entire wall is to be sided vertically, there is usually no need to check the side for squareness, that is, to measure the ends of the wall to make certain they are of equal height. Even if one end of the wall is a little higher than the other, no one is going to notice the slight angle across the tops of the vertical siding.

Cover the wall with perforated aluminum foil or core board, if you wish. Install ¾-inch corner posts, as described in the previous chapter.

This done, establish the bottom edge of the siding you are going to apply. Do this by nailing a J channel, with a suitable opening, across the bottom of the wall, but first drill ¼-inch holes 16 or so

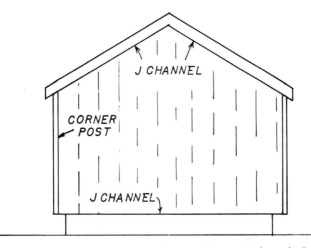

Basic arrangement of the various parts when installing vertical panels. Panel application can start at either side. Varying the width of the starting panel varies the position of the center panel.

inches apart across its bottom. The J channel produces the neatest appearance, since it hides the lower ends of the panels.

Ascend to the underside of the soffit or the rake trim. Nail a J channel to the wall, opening facing downward. If there is no more work to be done above the channel, position it about ¼ inch clear of the trim or soffit. If you plan to work there, it is best to give yourself at least 1 inch of clearance. Naturally this J channel's width is the channel across the bottom of the wall and suited to the panels you are going to use.

You now have lineal posts terminating the sides of your wall and J channels, facing each other, terminating the top and bottom of your wall. You have built out or not built out the house trim, as you have decided, and you have either covered the house trim or have painted it. But you have not yet applied channels or runners to the sides, bottoms, and tops of the doors and windows.

INSTALLING THE PANELS

The first panel. If the first vertical panel needs to be cut lengthwise, cut it. (Use a piece of test scrap as required.) Slide the panel into the corner post channel, with the nailing flange on the outside. Carefully examine the fit between the panel edge and the channel. If it is snug, or at least not flapping around, fine. You need do no more. If the fit is loose—and this will depend on the style of panel and if and where it has been cut lengthwise—the method most often used to tighten the joint consists of positioning a channel runner within the post channel and then sliding the panel edge into the channel runner.

Select the channel runner that fits your panel's side best. Cut the runner to a length ⅜ inch shorter than the distance from the inside bottom of the upper J channel, positioned atop the wall, to the inside bottom of the lower J channel, positioned across the wall's lower edge. Drill a ¼-inch hole near one end of the runner. Position the runner within the post channel. Lift the runner up

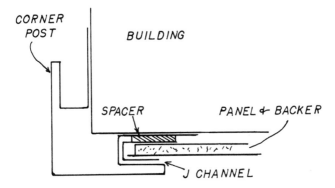

Cross-section view of how a J channel can be used inside a corner post to make the edge of a vertical panel and backer board fit more tightly. If desired, a spacer can be placed behind the J channel, as shown, to bring the front of the panel as far forward as possible, making for a neater joint.

against the upper J channel. Drive a nail through the hole you drilled. Now drive nails through the center of slots in the runner's flange; 1¼-inch nails will do.

If you examine the runner in the post, you will note that a small space exists between them. If you wish to eliminate this gap, you can fur the runner out by this distance before you nail it in place. Few professional applicators bother to do this. When the job is finished, this space is hardly noticeable.

If you need more than a single piece of runner, hang the second piece from a nail before you nail its flange down. The runner doesn't have to be continuous. It is out of sight.

Now, cut a vertical panel ¼ inch shorter than the distance between the inside bottoms of the two facing channels. Drill a ¼-inch hole 2 inches down from the panel's top end, at about the center of its width. Slide this panel into the channel runner that is within the post. Lift the panel as far as it will go. Drive a nail through the hole you drilled. Then drive nails through the slotted holes in the nailing flange.

If you require two panel sections to cover the height of the wall, hang the lower section first from a single nail, as described in the previous paragraph. Then nail it down. Then hang the upper section and nail it down. An overlap of an inch or so is plenty.

The second and following panels are installed just like the first. They all hang from a nail, which permits you to place the flange nails in the center of the slots and permits the panels to expand downward.

The last panel. When you come to the last panel, try a piece of scrap to see how the panel may fit. If necessary, cut the scrap experimentally first. Then slide the scrap into place and see how it fits within the corner post. You may or may not have to install a second channel runner here. If you do need a runner, install it as previously described. Then install the last panel.

Since there will be nothing but friction to keep the last panel from swinging sideways on its nail, it is advisable to drive a few stainless steel, self-tapping screws through the weep holes of the next-to-last panel's edge and into the last panel. If there are no holes here, drill them. Do not use the awl. One hole and screw every 2 vertical feet will be plenty.

DOOR AND WINDOW FRAME TREATMENT

The method used to fit vertical panels around a door and window frame is exactly the same as that used when applying horizontal siding. The only difference is that you will be placing the sides of the panels alongside the sides of the door and window frames. This simply means that you will be using ½- or ⅝-inch channels (whichever fits best) at the sides of the frames and the wider channels, beneath and above the frames.

VERTICAL PANELS BENEATH A GABLE ROOF

Everything is handled exactly the same as described for applying vertical panels to a rectangular or square wall, except that you have to fasten your J channels at an angle directly beneath the rake

Installing a J channel beneath the metal covering the fascia board on the rake end of a roof. To make a tight fit here, use a hammer with a small head and drive the nails through the bottom of the channel. The top ends of vertical panels will now be fitted into the channel after core board or furring strips have been nailed to the shakes. *Courtesy Buy Rite Siding Inc.*

trim or sloping eaves. The top ends of the panels have to be cut at an angle that conforms to the angle of the J channels. Follow the same program of hanging each panel from a single nail and cutting the panel ¼ inch short of the bottom channel.

Centering. If you simply start paneling at one side of the wall and work right across, you may or may not end up with one panel centered directly beneath the peak of the roof. If the sight of the center panel failing to line up with the peak of the roof will not disturb your esthetic sense, forget it. If it will, here is how you can make certain the panel is centered:

Start as before. Prepare your corner posts and top and bottom channels. Drop a plumb bob (a weight on a string will do equally well) from the center of the underside of the roof peak. Drive a nail into the wall alongside the top portion of the string and another near the bottom portion. Remove the plumb bob and snap a chalk line between the two nails. Now temporarily center the exposed portion of a vertical panel over the chalk line. Measure from the hook edge of the panel back to the corner. Divide this distance by the exposure of each panel. For example, if the distance into the post channel is 52 inches and you are going to use panels with 8 inches of exposure, dividing 52 by 8 gives you 6 with 4 inches left over. Thus the first panel has to have 4 inches of exposure. To be certain, cut the first panel out of a piece of scrap; then hang the rest of the panels temporarily in place and see how they come out. Correct the first panel as necessary.

The procedure is exactly as before. The only difference is that you start with a partial-width panel in order to properly locate the center panel.

COMBINING VERTICAL AND HORIZONTAL PANELS

The horizontal panels are installed first. The top edge of the panels terminate in a channel runner. A length of narrow-width drip edge, sometimes also called vertical base flashing, is nailed directly above the channel runner. The bottom edges of the vertical panels are aligned ¼ inch above this horizontal metal strip. If you wish, you can install a J channel above the vertical base flashing. This will hide the lower edges of the vertical panels and relieve you of the necessity of cutting the panels perfectly straight. Remember to drill drain holes in the bottom of the J channel. Don't omit the base flashing, as that acts to keep water out from behind the horizontal panels.

From here on up and across, the balance of the job is exactly as before.

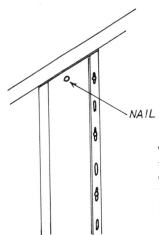

NAIL

Vertical panels are hung from a nail driven through a hole near their top. Then nails can be driven through the nailing holes in the nailing flange. In this way the panel holds its vertical position but is free to expand downward with increasing temperatures.

SLOPING PANELS

If you wish, you can slope the panels beneath a gable roof end. It is easier than it may appear to be. Use horizontal panels for the job. Start by nailing channel runners up near the underside of the rake trim or soffit. As before, leave just a little clearance. Next, drop a plumb bob from the underside of the roof's peak. Mark the position of the line on the side of the building. Install a J channel along the bottom horizontal edge of the wall. This channel can be at the bottom edge of the building or directly above horizontal siding. Its position is important only in that it serves to terminate the bottom edges of the sloped siding.

Install two lengths of J channel, back to back and centered over the vertical line coming down from the roof's peak. You now have a triangle, with the sides and bottom edge lined with channel runner and J channel. The triangle is divided into two equal sections by two vertical J channels.

Cut a piece of panel to fit one of the two corners formed by the vertical channels and the horizontal channel. Cut the metal so that

One way to treat a gable-end vent is to make louvers in the panels that are applied over the vent. These louvers are formed by a special tool, which can be rented or borrowed from some of the siding suppliers. *Courtesy Aluminum Association.*

the nailing flange is uppermost (at an angle, of course) and exactly parallel to the sloping surface of the roof on that half. Nail this triangle-shaped panel in place. From here on, you work your way upward, cutting the ends of the panels at an angle to conform to the confining channels. The last panel may have to be cut lengthwise to fit into the runner properly. Repeat the process on the other half of the gable.

Venting. If the gable end of the building is vented, construct a wood frame around the opening. Treat it as you treated the rest of the house trim and install siding right up to it and the same way you installed it up to the doors and windows.

As an alternative, you can use louvered panels over the building's vent openings. Use a lot more louver area than the house vent, since you will restrict air passage when you cover the vent with louvered panels.

8

Applying Vinyl Siding, Fascia, and Trim

Polyvinyl chloride siding, fascia, and trim is made by molding and extruding the thermoplastic into the desired shapes. At the present time, vinyl (or PVC, as it is sometimes called) siding and accessories are manufactured in six fairly pale colors, including white, with smooth and textured surfaces and in a number of different architectural styles. These include 8-inch and double–4-inch clapboard for horizontal application and various widths of beveled and board-and-batten siding for vertical installation.

Like its aluminum counterpart, vinyl formed-strip siding is manufactured by a number of companies, each with its own so-called system and somewhat differing nomenclature. However, so far as application is concerned, there is hardly a whit of difference between the installation of one plastic company's product and that of another. And, for almost all practical purposes, there is very little difference between applying plastic siding, fascia, soffit, and trim and aluminum siding, fascia, soffit, and trim.

Vinyl siding is sold by siding distributors who may also sell aluminum siding, roofing products, and even lumber.

Major data. The horizontal vinyl siding panels are made in 8-inch and double–4-inch panels that are usually 12 feet 6 inches long and 9 inches wide overall. The vertical panels are usually 9 inches wide overall and 10 feet long. One square (100 square feet of coverage) weighs about 45 pounds. Generally the panels are packed 2 squares to a carton. Panels for use on the soffit are usually 10 feet long with 7 inches of exposure. Generally they are not made in as many colors as the siding panels. Soffit panels may be solid or perforated. Plastic panels do not have weep holes along their edges, as do aluminum panels. The reason is that the plastic panels do not join one another as tightly as do the aluminum panels.

Since vinyl's coefficient of expansion is high, insulation is never cemented to the rear sides of the panels. Instead the panels are insulated in one of two other ways. Either the insulation is slipped

A few of the plastic accessories that are available to use with plastic panels. *Courtesy Society of the Plastics Industry, Inc.*

Three backer boards; fiberboard, polystyrene, and honeycomb. *Courtesy Society of the Plastics Industry, Inc.*

in behind the panels in the form of strips or sheet insulation is nailed over the entire wall first.

As with aluminum, "drop-in" strip insulation or the sheet insulation may be used. The strips are successively positioned behind the panels after the panel's bottom edge has engaged the starter strip or lower panel. Following that, the panel is nailed. That holds the insulation permanently in place. The sheet insulation is merely held in place by a few nails. The edges of the sheets are butted against one another. When the panels are nailed in place, the insulating sheets are there to stay.

For maximum insulation, perforated aluminum foil is nailed over the wall before any other insulation is used. Just a few small staples will hold the aluminum in place until you apply the siding.

Four types of insulation are presently used. The most effective is polystyrene foam, followed by foamed sheathing board, fiberboard, and lastly by honeycomb backerboard.

As with aluminum, either inside and outside corner posts or individual corners can be used. The uninsulated PVC panels will fit into posts having ¾-inch openings. The insulated panels require 1⅛-inch openings. In addition there are a considerable number of accessories to draw upon to help you assemble your siding, soffit, and fascia. There is a range of J channels with widths or openings from ⅜ inch to 1⅛ inch. There are starter strips, undersill and finishing trim, drip caps, vertical starter panels, frieze runners (F channels), batten strips, fascia covers, fascia corners, roof edging, rake edging, starter-divider strips, louvered panels, and more. In addition, solid vinyl is also sold in coil form, generally 9 inches wide and 150 inches long.

WORKING WITH PLASTIC

Plastic panels are light. A full panel weighs little more than 3 pounds. In cool weather the panels are rigid and easily handled by one man. In hot weather the panels become soft and limp. Unless you store the panels in a cool basement or cellar before bringing them out into the sun to apply them, it is best to have a second man on the far end of the panel. Otherwise, you will have difficulty installing it properly.

When the temperature of the vinyl is above freezing, you can easily cut it with tin snips and a knife. When the temperature goes down, the plastic becomes increasingly brittle and stiff. In answer to your question, "When is vinyl too cold to apply?" the answer is, when it is too cold for you to work outdoors.

You can circumvent the weather by storing the vinyl indoors where it is warm and by cutting the vinyl either indoors or immediately after you take it outside, before the plastic has had time to cool down.

However, you can cut vinyl at almost any temperature if you do not use the snip but cut it with a fine-tooth saw and support it well while cutting. Circular saw blades should be mounted in the reverse position. Their teeth should have no set. A little soap on the blade will ease cutting.

You can also drill vinyl at any temperature. Punching is another matter. The best way to find out how the plastic will respond is to try the punch—and the snips, too—on a piece of scrap. That will

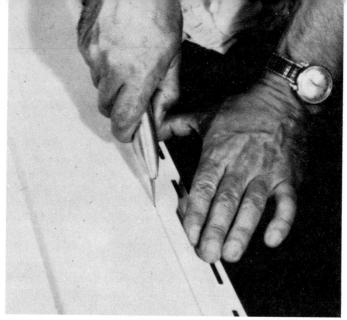

Using a razor knife to make a lengthwise cut on a plastic or vinyl panel. If you don't cut through, bend the panel along the score mark until it separates. *Courtesy Society of the Plastics Industry, Inc.*

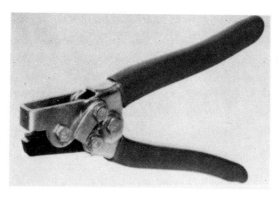

A snaplock punch. *Courtesy Society of the Plastics Industry, Inc.*

"clue" you much more rapidly and accurately than a thermometer.

You will find the plastic provided with nail holes for almost every contingency. However, if you need holes, drill ¼-inch holes for panel nails and ⅛-inch holes for trim nails. Do not try driving nails through cool plastic; you will surely shatter it.

Using a snaplock punch to expand the edge of a vinyl panel.
Courtesy Society of the Plastics Industry, Inc.

Basic rules of working with vinyl. Do not put tension on the panels by pulling them tightly against one another. Always leave a clearance of ¼ inch at a minimum between the end of a panel and the accessory that holds it. In other words, if the exact distance from the inside of one J channel to the other is exactly 12 feet, cut the panel to 11 feet 11½ inches. If you are applying the vinyl in cold weather, allow a minimum of ⅜ inch at each end for expansion. Place the nails in the center of the slots. *Do not drive the nails home.* Always leave about 1/32-inch clearance between the underside of the nailhead and the surface of the nailing slot. The panels must *hang* freely from the nails. The panels are *not nailed to the wall* in the usual sense of drive-home nailing. Do not face-nail if you can possibly help it. Since you cannot drive the nail home and since it must be in an oversized hole, face nails on plastic look far worse than face nails on metal.

Joints between plastic and plastic or plastic and wood are never caulked. The reason is plastic's large coeffecent of expansion. Because of this, the faying surfaces (meeting surfaces) of the joint move so much in response to temperature changes that no caulking would remain intact.

Using tinsnips to cut a plastic panel.

TOOLS

You will need a hammer, folding rules, tin snips or aviation snips (compound action snips), chalk line, razor knife, a fine-tooth handsaw for wood (sometimes called a finishing or trim saw) and/or a circular saw with a fine-toothed blade, a spirit level, and an electric drill with ¼- and ⅛-inch bits. As an alternative, you can use a punch that can make equal-size holes.

In addition you may need a snaplock punch. This tool looks like a large pair of pliers. It makes a pair of parallel cuts in the plastic, and at the same time it pushes the vinyl out from between the cuts to form a louver-shaped projection about ⅛ inch high. The projection expands the plastic and helps lock it in place within what might otherwise be loose-fitting trim. When you purchase or rent a snaplock punch, get one made for use with plastic.

Should you need to remove a panel, you will require an unlocking tool.

Using a hacksaw to cut a plastic outside corner.

DETERMINING QUANTITY OF MATERIAL REQUIRED

Measure up your building as previously outlined in Chapter 3. You will lose as much vinyl to unavoidable waste as you will lose aluminum, so use the same suggested figures. You will also need as many nails and, if you are going to use it, as much perforated aluminum foil.

APPLYING SOFFIT AND FASCIA

Prepare the building by removing the leaders, gutters, and associated hardware. Clean the soffit and fascia of loose paint. Paint the bare spots. Fill the cracks with putty. Tighten all loose boards.

Soffit supports. Nail an F channel (GAF) or a soffit channel (Celotex) to the bottom edge of the fascia. Place a long spirit level against the bottom of the channel and against the wall at one end of the fascia. Adjust the level until the bubble is centered, and mark the spot where the top of the level touches the building. Repeat at the other end of the fascia. Then snap a chalk line between the two marks you have made on the wall. Next nail either a second F channel or a second soffit channel directly above the chalk line. You now have two channels facing one another across the width of your soffit. The channels are horizontal, parallel, equidistant above the ground, and equidistant from one another for their entire length.

Paneling the soffit. If the spacing between the soffit channels is no wider than a soffit panel, you can slip panels in along the length of the space. If the space is narrower than a panel, the panel can be trimmed. Panel ends can be overlapped, or they can be joined by using two J channels back to back to make an H-shaped support. If the spacing is wider than a single panel, cut the panel into short lengths and fit the pieces across the space between the facing supporting channels. The side edges of the soffit panels interlock.

When you have to go around a corner, follow the suggestion given in Chapter 4 and use two J channels back to back for the diagonal joint.

To provide ventilation, use perforated soffit panels near or directly beneath the louvers in an existing soffit.

Covering the fascia. If at this point you have some sort of channel nailed to the bottom edge of the fascia board, measure the vertical width of the fascia board and add the width of the channel. If not, use the width of the fascia board alone as your measurement. Select a fascia cover, also called fascia panel, as wide as your measurement or wider. If wider, cut the fascia cover's width down to match. Next, if the fascia goes around a corner, select a fascia corner to fit, or use a larger corner and cut its vertical width to fit. Face-nail the plastic corners in place. A few 1-inch aluminum nails will do.

Nail finishing trim along the top edge of the fascia board, just beneath the roof shingle overhang. Now, use the snaplock and punch the top edge of the fascia cover every 6 inches. (Celotex calls theirs a fascia cover. GAF calls theirs a fascia panel.) Push the punched edge of the fascia cover up into the trim and push the bottom edge of the cover—the edge with the channel—over the bottom edge of the fascia *and* whatever channel may be nailed to the bottom of the fascia board. No nails are used.

To join fascia covers, overlap them by about 2 inches. Cut the channel portion of one cover back 2½ inches before overlapping. (The extra ½ inch permits the panels to expand.) The balance of the accessories are merely installed end to end with at least ¼ inch of clearance between ends.

The fascia covers go over the fascia corners and just rest there. Incidentally, if you cannot purchase fascia corners to match your requirements, you can bend them out of vinyl coil stock. Use a regular brake. Overbend, because the plastic will rebound a little, and make certain the plastic's temperature is above freezing or it may crack.

To cover rake fascia, where there is no soffit, install finishing trim along the top edge of the rake fascia just under the roof shingle overhang. Then use a fascia cover cut to fit. Use the snaplock punch on its edge as before. Then push the cover up into place.

COVERING THE HOUSE TRIM

Start as previously suggested and try the channels alongside the house trim, meaning the frames around your doors and windows, to see whether or not you want to build the trim out. Use the ¾-inch J channel when you are not using drop-in insulation. Use the $1\frac{1}{16}$-inch channel when you are. Position a section of channel having the correct opening width next to the side of a door or window if you are going to apply horizontal siding there. Position the channel above the window or door if you are going to apply vertical siding to that area.

If you do not want to build the trim out, just paint it and forget it. If you build the trim out, it is best to cover it with either aluminum or vinyl rather than paint it.

Aluminum, in colors to match or contrast that of the balance of the siding, is frequently used to cover house trim when the house is sided with plastic. The reason is that aluminum is much easier to work with. It can be bent more sharply. You can start nail holes in aluminum with an awl, whereas you should always drill holes for all nails to be driven through vinyl. When necessary, you can caulk aluminum joints. You can't caulk vinyl joints because temperature changes always open them.

Covering the trim with vinyl. First, check out your supplier. Some of the siding manufacturers make a large variety of accessories, including some that will fit directly over your house trim. There is no point in making trim covering if you can purchase it already made.

What cannot be covered with preformed vinyl can be covered by bending vinyl in a standard brake to fit over the wood trim. Use coil stock. Make certain its temperature is above freezing, and overbend because it will straighten a bit after you release it from the brake.

As with aluminuhm, the sill is always covered first, followed by the vertical side pieces. The top of the frame is covered last. Use 1¼-inch aluminum nails and drill holes for them. Drive the nails snug, but take care not to lock the plastic beneath the nailheads. The plastic must be able to move a little with temperature changes.

If you end up with small openings between the ends of the pieces of vinyl, don't caulk them, since with the passage of time the chances are that the opening will look worse with the caulking than it would without it.

PREPARING THE BUILDING

Remove all the shutters, mailboxes, flower boxes, and the like. Cut off any projecting boards and nail the balance of the boards firmly in place.

Use a small saw and cut the ends off the windowsills and door-sills to make them flush with the side frames.

Examine the sides of the building to determine whether the walls are flat or have hollows and/or bulges. Any hollow or bulge of less than 1 inch in 20 feet or so of wall can be ignored. Greater deviations must be corrected. Siding will not hide a deformation in a wall.

Hollows can usually be corrected by installing furring strips or straps to build the low spot out. Space the wood strips so that they fall in line with the nail holes in the siding.

Bulges can be corrected by actually cutting the wall back at its high spots or by building the rest of the wall out. Generally it is easier and better to cut than build. Remember, little is lost if you have to remove some of the old siding, because you are going to cover the areas with insulation and siding.

CHECKING FOR SQUARENESS

Measure carefully from the bottom of every building corner up to its top and note the measurements. All corners must be equal in height. If one or more is shorter than the rest, make them all even by extending the short corners. Do this by nailing a bottom board to the lower side of the building at the necessary angle. A length of ⅜-inch plywood 6 or more inches wide is fine. If you don't take this precaution, you will end up having to cut the top hori-zontal panel at an angle, and it will look poorly.

PROVIDE A FLAT SUPPORTING SURFACE

Everything that has been said concerning the need to provide a flat nailing surface for aluminum siding in Chapter 6, applies equally to working with plastic siding.

APPLYING HORIZONTAL VINYL SIDING

Start by nailing a starter strip along the bottom edge of the building, either onto the building itself or onto a bottom board. The starter strip should start 3 inches short of an outside corner if you are going to use a lineal corner post. If not, position the end of the starter strip 1 inch away from an outside corner. End the starter strip 3 inches away from all inside corners, and position the bottom edge of the strip about ¼ inch above the lower edge of the building or bottom board.

Foil and insulation. Cover the side of the building with perforated foil and follow the sheet insulation if you are not going to drop strips behind the panels.

Installing the accessories. First nail the corner posts in place, assuming that you are going to use them. Start by drilling a ¼-inch hole 2 inches down from the top of the first post and through the middle of each nailing flange. Position the corner against the building, the top end of the post as high as you want it to go. If there is a finished surface above the post end, ¼ inch of clearance is fine. If you have to do work above the post end, use your judgment as to the amount of clearance you will need.

Next, nail the post in place by driving 1½-inch aluminum nails partway through the drilled holes. These two nails carry the weight of the post. All thermal expansion will be downward. Now, if the corner post is not long enough to reach to the bottom of the wall, measure and cut another section of corner post 2 inches longer than the required length. Position the second corner post against the building. Slip the top inch or so *beneath* the in-place corner post. Adjust the second post vertically until its bottom end is approximately ½ inch below the edge of the house frame. Next, drill two ¼-inch holes through the flanges of the second corner post accessory. Position these holes ½ inch below the bottom end of the in-place, upper post. Drive nails partway through the drilled holes. Now you have two corner posts hanging from two pairs of nails. Push the lower post against the building and nail it in place using 1¼-inch nails. Do the same with the top post. Place the nails in the center of their slots. *Do not drive the nails home.*

Nail J channels to the sides of the door and window frames. Use channels with ¾-inch openings for plain siding and channels with 1⅛-inch openings when you are going to install drop-in insulation. Nail drip caps over each door and window frame. Hold off nailing the undersill trim in place until you know whether or not you will have to build out beneath the sill to hold the panel properly.

Applying the siding. Measure the panels and cut them ¼ inch short of the bottom of the channels in each post. Hold the panel in place and lift it lightly upward until its lower edge engages the interlock. Then nail it, described just above. Remember, keep the nails in the center of the slots; do not pull upward on the panels and do not drive the nails home.

When you have to fit short panels between channels, bow the panels to slip them in.

When you come to a doorway or window, measure the tab that has to be cut out. Cut it. Position the cut panel and see whether or not you need to fur out and how much. Then install the undersill trim nailed upside down (nailing flange up). Generally, you do not have to snap-lock the edge of the plastic that fits into the undersill trim. But if the fit is loose, it helps.

Continue on up until you reach the top of the wall. Install under-

A

Steps in applying vinyl panels to a clapboard wall.

A. The corner post is nailed in place.

B. A nail through the top of the post keeps it from falling. Nails through the nailing slots—one every couple of feet—hold the post in place. Note the space beneath the nail head.

C. The starting strip is nailed to the bottom edge of the lowest clapboard. The thin spacer that was used is not visible in the picture.

D. Since the nailing flange on the panel will fall atop an indentation, a strip of lath is nailed in place to provide a flat supporting surface.

B

C

D

E.

E. The first panel is lifted up against the nailing strip and slid into place. At least 1/4 inch of clearance is left between the end of the panel and the inside surface of the corner post.

F. A finer backer board is slipped behind the panel.

G. The panel is nailed to the wall. If you keep the nail heads flush with the ridge along the nailing slots, you will not drive the nails in too deeply. That is the purpose of the ridge.

H. The "factory" end of a vinyl panel. Note how far back the nailing flange has been cut—almost 2 inches. The pencil mark indicates the desirable overlap to be used when joining panels. Holding the lapped end to this mark will leave about 1 inch of space between the nailing flanges on the two panels, which is necessary to allow for thermal expansion.

F.

I. The second panel is positioned.

J. The second panel is lifted to make certain it fully engages the in-place panel's interlock or hook.

sill trim there, measure the panel, and cut as necessary. Again, snaplock punch or not as required.

Vinyl panels are joined end to end by lapping. Generally, an inch or so of overlap is plenty. But no matter how much you lap, always cut one nailing flange back a sufficient distance to leave ½ inch of space between nailing flange ends. The factory ends (panel ends as they come from the factory) are cut this way.

Individual corners are positioned by sliding them up and over the ends of the two panels that meet at a corner. The two panel ends must be ¼ inch clear of the edge of the building corner. The corner accessory must lock fully into the two panel interlocks. The single nail that holds the corner must not be driven home.

INSTALLING VERTICAL SIDING

Start by installing corner posts having suitable openings for the panels you are going to use. Prepare a J channel by drilling ¼-inch holes, 12 inches apart, through its bottom for drainage. Nail this channel across the bottom of the wall after cutting it to a length ¼ inch short of each corner post. As an alternative you can use a drip cap in place of the channel.

Next, you can install J channels of suitable size just below the eaves or gable rakes. The top ends of the panels fit into these channels. If any of the windows or doors do not have drip caps, install them now. Use some scrap to help you determine whether or not the J channels beneath the sills need to be furred out. Then install the J channels, with or without furring as you deem necessary. Let the sides and tops of the windows go until later.

Now, if you are going to apply panels to a square or rectangular area, temporarily position one vertical panel with its slotted end within the slot in a post. Use this as a guide and position a vertical starter strip alongside. (Note that the vertical starter strip comprises two interlocks facing in opposite directions. Your starter strip will actually be the second panel out from the corner post.) Next, cut the first vertical panel to its proper length, which should be a full ⅜ inch short of the distance between the J channel on top and the J channel on the bottom. In other words, when positioned (and nailed), the first vertical panel and all the other panels should be ⅜ inch short of the inside bottom surface of the horizonal support.

Next, drill a ¼-inch hole through the middle of the panel's width about 2 inches down from the top. Place the insulation behind the panel. Slip the panel into the post slot. Then lift the panel all the way up into the channel. Drive a nail through the hole you drilled. Stop when the nail head is ¹⁄₃₂ inch short of the panel face. You now have a panel hanging from a nail. Position the starter strip, making certain it fully engages the first panel. Drill a hole through top of the starter strip. Lift the strip into position. Nail to the wall. Now, position the necessary nails in the middle of the nail slots on both sides of the starter strip. (You will have to remove the first vertical strip to do so.) Then replace the first strip and work your way across the wall, hanging each panel on a nail, the panel end ¼ inch clear of the inside bottom of the bottom support.

If you are going to side beneath a gable and want your starter panel to be directly underneath the peak of the roof, drop a plumb line (weight on a string) from the gable and center your vertical starter on this line. When you do this, you side in two directions from the starter strip.

Naturally, if the roof above your vertical panels slopes, you have to cut the top ends of the panels to match.

Finishing up. Let us assume for the moment that you are not going to hit a window or door before you hit a corner post. So, when you come to the final panel, you may have to cut it lengthwise to fit into the post slot. When you cut, cut it about ¼ inch short. Now try fitting the edge into the post slot. If it fits snugly because of insulation, etc., fine. If it doesn't, slip a length of undersill trim into the post slot. Shim or fur the trim out so that it is just behind the front surface of the post. Nail the trim into place. Now, snaplock the edge of the vertical siding panel and slip it into place.

Alternate starting method. In the method just described you start your vertical paneling with a corner post followed by a panel followed by a vertical starter strip. You can, if you wish, eliminate the vertical starter strip.

Start instead with a panel, as before. If this panel fits snugly (nailing flange outside the post), fine. If not, slide a J channel or a length of undersill trim into the slot in the post—whichever accessory makes for a better fit. If necessary, snaplock the siding edge that enters the post. But remember, make the joint no tighter than a snug fit. If you jam the parts together, you will have trouble when the vinyl expands with the summer's heat.

Vertical panels are joined by overlapping, just like horizontal vinyl panels. Just don't forget to cut the flange back so that there is a ½ inch of space between one flange end and the next.

Windows and doors. Cut the panel as may be necessary to fit alongside the window or door. Use whatever J channel width fits best. Then, as previously described, slip a length of undersill trim inside the channel and fur it out, if necessary.

9

Siding Repairs

As stated previously, bent aluminum siding panels disturb the esthetic sense but little else. The panels remain as watertight and as heat-retaining as before. However, if your esthetic senses are offended and you don't mind the effort, here is how to repair damaged panels:

REPLACING A CORNER POST

Use a razor knife and make two long, continuous score marks down the length of the damaged corner. Use a pair of pliers and break the aluminum along your score marks. Then make two more score marks along the inside of the post where the metal folds over the ends of the panels. Again, bend the metal back and forth until it breaks. You now have two aluminum angles nailed to the wall.

Take a new length of lineal corner post. Cut its return bends off. Spread it a little and slip it over the remains of the old corner post. Push it into place. Then use an awl to make a starting dimple and follow with an electric drill and make a few holes through both the new and old metal. If you don't use the awl, the drill will

118

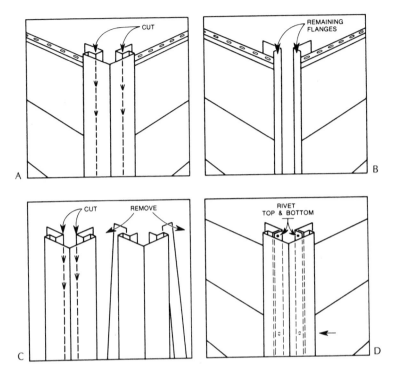

One way to replace a damaged aluminum corner post.

A. Score the damaged post as shown with a razor knife.

B. Use pliers to break the metal along the score marks leaving two flanges as shown.

C. Remove the nailing flanges from a new corner post, as shown.

D. Place the new post over the old, in-place flanges. Drill holes through both flanges and rivet one to the other. *Courtesy Aluminum Association.*

skip around and scratch the paint. Use self-tapping metal screws to lock the new post to the old. One screw every 2 feet is plenty.

An alternate method consists of leaving the old post in place after making certain it is straight and doesn't bulge outward. Prepare the new post by cutting its return flanges off. Slip it atop the old, in-place post and fasten it with self-tapping screws. In warm weather you can use epoxy cement between the two posts to hold the outer post in place.

REPLACING A DAMAGED PANEL

Start by cutting the damaged panel lengthwise down its middle for a distance a few inches beyond the section that is damaged. Remove and discard the damaged section.

Remove the top lock—the edge that has the long nailing holes—from a piece of new panel. Run your razor knive across the panel beneath the top lock. Then bend it back and fourth until you break it off.

Next, try the new piece of panel over the bare area. See if it fits snugly and looks reasonably well. Then remove the repair panel

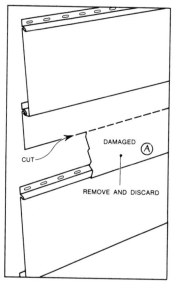
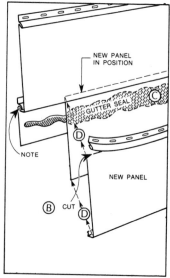

How to replace damaged aluminum panels.
A. Cut the panel with a razor knife and remove.
B. Remove the nailing flange and top lock or hook from a good panel.
C. Apply gutter seal or a similar cement to the surface of the old, cut panel.
D. Slip the new, cut panel up and into place. Press it firmly against the sealing material to hold it there. And drive some stainless steel self-tapping screws up through the weep holes in the bottom of the new panel, into the in-place panel to be certain the new panel remains in place. *Courtesy Aluminum Association.*

and smear a layer of gutter seal or epoxy cement across the old panel above the hole. Replace the patch and press it firmly into place. The seal or the cement will hold it there.

These two repair suggestions will, of course, not remedy all possible damage, but they do illustrate the general approach: You don't really remove the in-place metal, you cover it with new. With a little ingenuity you should have little difficulty taking care of whatever comes up

REPAIRING DAMAGED VINYL SIDING

To repair a damaged vinyl panel you must remove it. This is accomplished with the aid of an unlocking tool, available at the siding supplier. Use the tool to disengage the interlock of the panel above the broken panel. Pull the lower portion of the higher panel free, while you use a hammer to remove the nails from the damaged panel. Replace the damaged panel and reengage it with the above and lower panels.

To replace a damaged corner post you have first to remove all of the adjacent panels. With horizontal siding this may result in the loss of 10 to 20 percent of the panels. The alternative is to cut off the nailing flanges from a section of a matching corner post and slip it over the damaged section. A couple of small self-tapping screws will hold it in place.

When the weather is warm, you might try some of the epoxy cements on the damaged portions of the siding; it's worth a try. Roughen the surfaces to be cemented first. Apply the cement and then the patch.

PART TWO

Roofing

Asphalt shingles make an attractive, long-lasting roof surface. *Courtesy Asphalt Roofing Manufacturers Association*

10

Introduction to Asphalt Shingle Roofing

Asphalt shingle roofing is used on 95 percent or more of all the pitched-roof residential buildings in this country. You can see this roofing everywhere, in many colors and color combinations, even in pure white.

There is good reason for this. Asphalt shingles are the least expensive roofing material available that is also attractive. It is also the easiest to install. It is fireproof to a considerable degree, verminproof, rotproof, and can last twenty-five years or more depending on the weight of the shingles applied. Furthermore, a second layer of shingles can be nailed atop the first without difficulty.

Asphalt shingles are relatively inexpensive. Generally the cost of the roofing material alone is under 33 percent of the usual labor-and-material roofing bid you may receive from a local contractor. If this appears to be unreasonable, bear in mind that he carries a load of about 21 percent in the form of insurance—compensation, unemployment, F.I.C.A., and liability—before he even begins to think about the time lost in coffee breaks, vacations, the cost of advertising, bookkeeping, office, truck, bad debts (contractors don't win all the time), and begins to think about wages for his crew and a profit for himself. Therefore, the financial reward for doing your own roofing can be considerable.

The actual work is not unpleasant and is quite simple. After you have nailed down a few dozen shingles, it will become almost automatic. Roofing doesn't take much time. It all depends on the complexity of the job. On an easy or simple job the average experienced roofer can lay down 1 square, which means 100 square feet of roofing in the trade, in an hour or two. On a difficult job, a job involving lots of dormers and other changes in roof direction requiring considerable cutting and flashing, the usual rate is about 1 square in two to three hours. An inexperienced person should be able to roof the average home in a week or so without trying very hard. One pertinent point to remember is that it isn't necessary to work continuously. A roof can be re-covered over a series of weekends.

WHEN TO REROOF

As asphalt shingles grow older, they lose their mineral coating, the layer of finely crushed particles of stone that help them resist weathering. You will find more and more of these particles in the house gutters, and when the shingles are in their last useful year, they begin to curl up and turn a lighter shade of brown at the edges. It is best not to wait too long after this happens, since a curled shingle will not stop the rain and will usually make laying a new roof on top more difficult.

Wood shingles get darker with age as rot gradually settles in. However, if the darker color doesn't trouble your esthetic sense, there is no need to do anything until the wind carries some of the weakened shingles away and the rain begins to join you in the living room. When this happens, it is the pan brigade or a new roof.

When the shingles lose their mineralized surface, it is time to reroof. *Courtesy Asphalt Roofing Manufacturers Association.*

ROOFING MATERIALS

Shingles. There are possibly a dozen different types of asphalt shingles currently manufactured. Of these the most popular are the

> three-tab strip shingle,
> T-lock shingle,
> two- and three-tab hexagon shingle,
> individual lock-down shingle,
> individual staple-down shingle,
> giant individual American shingle, and
> giant individual Dutch lap shingle.

Since you can pass through town after town in most of this country and see nothing but strip shingles on the roofs of the houses you pass, and since this shingle can be used for almost all roofs, only the application of this shingle is covered in detail in this book. However, the general principles of installation discussed here are applicable to all types of asphalt shingles. If you want to use other types of shingles, refer to the directions and accompanying drawings usually provided on shingle packages of all types.

Strip shingles can be applied to all roofs having a pitch of more than 4 inches in 12 (4/12) and less than 8 inches in 12 (8/12). When the roof's pitch is between 4/12 and 2/12, you can use strip shingles provided you underlay the shingles with watertight roll roofing (see Chapter 16) and either use strip shingles having self-sealing tabs or cement each tab down with a daub of roofing cement. It also helps with such a low pitch to lay the shingles 4 inches to the weather (meaning area exposed) instead of the usual 5 inches.

When the pitch is more than 1/12 and less than 2/12, you can use roll roofing. (Roll roofing is discussed near the end of this secton of the book.)

When the pitch is less than 1/12, it is best to use built-up roofing, which consists of roll roofing material completely sealed in place with some type of roofing cement. This is beyond the scope of this book.

When the pitch is greater than 8/12 (6/12 would be a 45-degree angle), ordinary strip roofing shingles cannot be used in the ordinary manner. Since this kind of roof is very rare on American homes, this type of roofing, like the built-up roofing, is not covered in this book.

Strip shingles are sold in packages. Depending on the weight of the shingles, there may be three, four, or five packages to a square. A square in roofing parlance means sufficient shingles to cover 100 square feet of roof surface properly.

Three-tab strips are always 36 inches long and 12 inches wide and are designed for a 5-inch exposure. This means that a 5-inch-wide, 36-inch-long area of each shingle is normally exposed to the

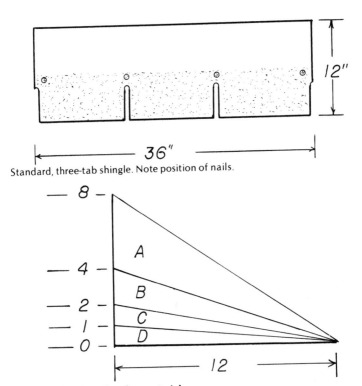

Standard, three-tab shingle. Note position of nails.

Guide to selection of roofing material.

A. When the roof's pitch is between 4 and 8 inches in 12, you can use strip shingles on top of 15 pound felt, laid dry.

B. When the roof's pitch is between 2 and 4 inches in 12, you can use strip shingles if you lay them on top of sealed (watertight) roll roofing.

C. When the roof's pitch is between 1 and 2 inches in 12, you can use roll roofing that is sealed.

D. When the pitch is 1 or less than 1 inch in 12, you must use built-up roofing.

weather. The balance of the shingle is covered by the following shingle. You can expose a little more if you wish, but a portion of the area that is not to be exposed is not mineralized, meaning it is not covered with fine particles of stone (which provide the color). So this limits the area that can be exposed. The roof will also be a little weaker, since there will be less shingle on the roof, so it is foolish to try to save on material by exposing much more than 5 inches.

Most manufacturers offer shingles in three weights. Some offer a choice of four shingle weights, which usually range from 205 to 380 pounds per square. This is literally the weight of the shingles and is directly related to their life expectancy. Typically a manufacturer will warranty his shingles ten to twenty-five years in direct relation to their weight. Generally the 235-pound shingle is guaranteed for fifteen years. The 300- to 325-pound shingle is guaranteed for twenty-five years.

At this writing the 235-pound shingle costs about $20 per square. The 300- to 325-pound shingle goes for about $40 per square.

The heavier shingles naturally require much more effort to lug up onto the roof. (The use of a rope and pulley is discussed in a following section.) However, the squares of heavy shingles are broken into more packages. Since the normal life of the very heavy shingles is 2½ times greater than the life of the lightest shingles, it is penny-wise and dollar-foolish to install the lightweight or even mediumweight shingles. Besides, you will also have to reroof fewer times over your lifespan (or the lifespan of the house—whichever is greater).

In addition to different weights, shingles are also offered in a variety of colors, color combinations, and textures.

Textured shingles are a bit heavier than the others, usually cost a little more, and usually must be installed in a slightly different but specific pattern to produce the desired appearance of wood shingles. The exact pattern to follow is always supplied on the package.

The dark, variegated colors are best for a number of reasons. The shingle itself is a tar and fiber combination that is black or very close to black. The color you see from the ground (the surface color) is that of the fine particles of colored stone pressed into the surface of the shingle proper. With time, the stones loosen and fall away. When this happens—and it always happens—the shingle loses color. If the surface color is light, the change is more marked than if the surface color is dark. In addition, the shingles do not lose their protective coating of stone evenly. Therefore an originally light-colored roof will look worn and shabby years before it has outlived its usefulness and years before a dark roof of equal quality looks bad.

There are also reasons for selecting variegated or mixed colors rather than solid colors, even if they are dark, and the reasons are not esthetic. When the color of the shingles on a roof is perfectly solid, it is much easier to see imperfections in shingle placement than when the shingle colors waver a bit—fluctuate, as it were—between deep blue and very deep blue or black. The eye is deceived, and it is difficult visually to delineate the lines formed by the edges of the shingles. Therefore if this is going to be your first time up on a roof, choose the color that will partially relieve you of the need for spacing the shingles perfectly.

Another reason is that integral color variations tend to hide color variations that result from aging. Remember, a shingle is good and useful so long is it keeps out the rain. So why let a color change force you to replace a roof before it has outlived its usefulness.

Strip shingles are normally delivered to the job on pallets. The shingles can be left to the weather as long as necessary.

Now we come to the white versus black argument: Which is cooler, which is warmer? White is cooler in the sun. It reflects more light and heat than does black. However, black radiates more heat than white. Thus, from an ideal point of view, you should have a white roof in the daytime when the sun is out and a black roof at night—in the summertime. In the winter you would want the reverse in order to absorb as much heat from the sun during the day and lose as little as possible at night. In this sad way we come to the end of the argument: Neither white nor black is best all the time. (A lot of the manufacturers are now putting mica in their dark-colored shingles. The mica helps reflect sunlight, giving these shingles all the advantages of the dark color and some of the advantage of the white.)

11

Materials and Tools
for Shingling a Roof

COMPUTING SHINGLE QUANTITY

There are a number of reasons why it is advisable—necessary even—to compute the number of shingles you need for a roof before you start the job. One reason is that many suppliers will not accept returned shingles even if the bundles have not been opened. Another is that suppliers do run out of shingles, and the following shipment they receive may not contain shingles that match perfectly to the shingles you already have in place. Another, perhaps less important, reason is that you may want to know your total costs before you start. If your experience with local contracting bids is similar to that of many other people, you cannot depend on their estimated shingle quantities. They vary too much from one contractor to another. And it is best to get *all* your shingles up on the roof before you start working so that you will not have to walk over newly laid shingles while you are loaded with bundles.

Measuring a gable roof. Measuring up a roof to determine necessary shingle quantity is not at all difficult. If you are going to shingle a gable roof, measure from eave to eave (where the gut-

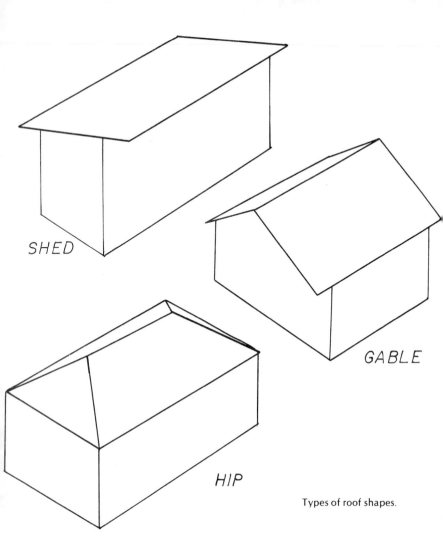

SHED

GABLE

HIP

Types of roof shapes.

ters are or should be) and then from rake (the side or edge of the roof that climbs from the eave to the ridge) to rake. Use a steel tape if you have one. It is more accurate and much easier to use than a folding rule for this kind of work. Then multiply one measurement by the other to find the number of square feet. Divide by 100 to find the number of squares. Each square, of course, requires three or more bundles. If the final figure results in

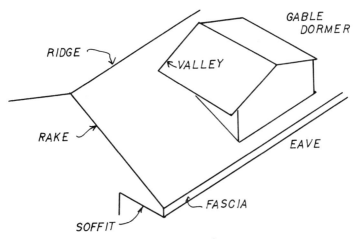

RIDGE

GABLE
DORMER

VALLEY

RAKE

EAVE

FASCIA

SOFFIT

The names of the more common parts of a roof.

a partial bundle, round it off by making the fractional bundle a full bundle.

As an example, if the roof is 40 feet by 52 feet, the square footage is 2,080, which divided by 100 becomes 20.8 squares. Rounding off brings it to 21 squares.

The first course of shingles, the course that is nailed in place just above the eaves, is always doubled. This can be accomplished by using one shingle atop the other for the first course or using

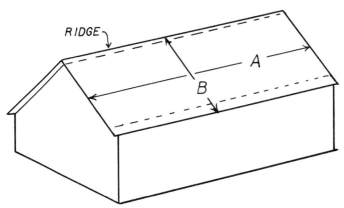

RIDGE

A

B

The area of the visible half of this roof is found by multiplying A by B.

a strip of special roofing called a starting roll. If we use the starting roll, which is easier and better, we need the combined length of the two eaves—in this case a total of 80 feet. If we use shingles, we can figure 80 shingles (any weight) to a square. Laid end to end, they would make a row 240 feet long. Thus we would need ⅓ square of shingles for the starters.

This leaves the ridge, which is 40 feet long. By rule of thumb, 1 square of shingles will cover 90 lineal feet of ridge. Thus, we would need a little less than ½ square of shingles for the ridge.

Adding everything up, we get:

> 21 squares for the roof itself
> ⅓ square for the starters
> ½ square for the ridge
> 21 ⅚ squares, which when rounded comes to 22 squares

To take care of waste, this figure is multiplied by 105 percent, which brings the total to 23.1 squares. We can drop the 0.1. Total requirement for this particular roof should be 23 squares of roofing shingles.

Let us consider a hip roof, which is slightly more difficult to measure. This type of a roof consists of four surfaces pitched towards a single ridge. Two surfaces are triangles. To measure their areas you measure straight down from the ridge to the eave and multiply this figure by the length of the eave, then multiply by ½ to get the area of that triangular surface.

The other two surfaces are trapezoids. The easy way to compute the area of a trapezoid is to break it up into a rectangle (or square) and two triangles. The area of a rectangle is its height times its width. The area of a triangle, as explained, is its height multiplied by one-half of the base length.

The accompanying illustrations show how easily all this is done. (If you are using a pocket computer, convert inches to fractions of a foot. For example, 2 inches equals 0.166 foot, found by dividing 2 by 12.)

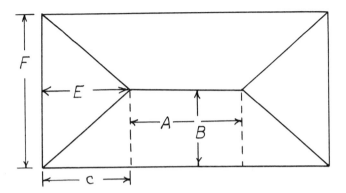

To calculate the area of a hip roof such as this, divide it into sections as shown. The square or rectangular section is found by multiplying A by B. The area of the triangular section adjoining is found by multiplying C by B times ½. The end section, which is also a triangle, is found by multiplying F by E times ½.

Measuring valleys. Now we have to consider roofs with valleys. A valley is formed by the junction of two or more gable-ended roof sections or of a gable dormer with a roof section. Since the ends of the shingles that lie adjacent to the valley must be cut off at an angle, valleys cause the waste of a portion of the shingles. To estimate this loss, figure each valley to be 1½ feet wide. Multiply the length of the valley by this figure to find the additional number of square feet of roofing needed to make up for the loss. Naturally all the valley areas have to be added to the total roof area.

Measuring dormers. Shingle quantity for gable dormers are computed almost exactly as described for gable roofs. Just remember that each gable dormer has a ridge, two roof sections, two lengths of starter edging, *and two valleys*.

A shed dormer has a single-section roof (all in one plane), and it is no problem to figure its shingle needs quickly. Just remember that roofs with a pitch of less than 4/12 require special treatment. This is discussed in Chapter 16.

ADDITIONAL MATERIALS

You will need nails and—for a new roof or a stripped old roof—an underlay of 15-pound roofing felt. Compute the felt requirement on the basis of roof area proper and add 15 percent to take care of waste and side overlap. The standard roll contains 400 square feet plus a 2-inch allowance for top lap.

Don't use 30-pound felt in place of 15 for underlaying strip shingles on a 4/12 or greater pitch on the assumption that a better job will result. Most likely the results will not be better. Roofing felt has a tendency to swell in the heat and wrinkle. This is much more pronounced with the thicker felt. The result may be an uneven finished surface. Normally water will not penetrate properly installed shingles. So the use of double-weight felt is a waste of time and money.

Also, do not use 15-pound (or any other weight) felt on top of old roofing, since the felt is apt to buckle and cause the new roof to rise in many places.

You will need 4 roofing nails per shingle strip. This works out to 320 nails per square. But since you will drop nails and some bundles contain 27 shingles, you had best figure 350 nails per square.

Always use galvanized roofing nails. Never use bare roofing nails. They will rust.

Use 1¼-inch nails on new work, 1¾-inch nails when the new roof is going over a single layer of old asphalt shingle roofing, and longer nails when there are two layers of asphalt shingles or wood shingles beneath the new roofing. Choose a nail length that will penetrate ¾ inch into the roof deck. There is no need for nails to go through the roof deck; in fact it is much better all around if they do not.

Depending on the type of job you are going to do and the shape and condition of the roof—whether it is new or old—you may need additional roofing materials. These materials are discussed as their need arises.

TOOLS

You will need a hammer, folding rule, hook knife (sometimes called carpet knife) or razor knife, some means for sharpening either of these knives, and a chalk line for all roofing work. If you are going to work with metal, you will need a pair of tin snips, and if you are going to work with wood, you will need a small cross-cut saw.

A word about the chalk line. You can use a length of mason's line, which is simply strong string, and dip it in chalk before you use it. Or you can purchase an encased chalk line. This device consists of a small metal case in which there is a reel wound with line and colored chalk. When you unwind the line, it is automatically covered with chalk.

These are the tools you will need to work with once you are up on the roof. To get up on the roof and stay there you will need a ladder. If the roof starts more than 15 feet above the ground, you may prefer a scaffold. If the roof's pitch is steep, you should not depend on the friction of your shoes alone to hold you up there; instead you should install a pair of roof jacks (sometimes called roof scaffolds). The jacks support one or two 2- by 6-inch planks, which should be free of knots and no more than 10 feet long. In addition, you will need a handful of 12-penny common nails to secure the packs to the roof. Ladders, scaffolds, and jacks are discussed in Chapter 17.

12

Shingling a New Roof

PREPARATION

Start by sweeping the entire roof clean with a broom. Then carefully go over the entire roof area and make certain there are no projecting nails or splinters sticking up.

If the gutters that are to be installed are the type that hang from straps nailed atop the roof deck, install them now, otherwise you will later have to lift the shingles to install them.

Side drip reducers. Some homeowners reduce the quantity of rainwater that would otherwise drip from the rake edges of the roof by using beveled siding to raise these edges. If you want to do this, simply nail ordinary beveled siding (pine is fine) along the edges of the roof, thick side nearest the rake. Start the siding 2 inches higher than the lower edge of the roof (eave) and stop the siding about 5 inches short of the ridge. Most homeowners (or is it home builders?) do not bother with this.

Bringing the material up. Bring everything you believe you will need up on the roof. Place the material clear of the first 6 feet of roof, where you will start to lay shingles, and spread the bundles over the roof according to where you judge you will need them.

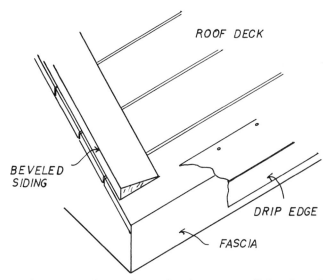

ROOF DECK

BEVELED
SIDING

DRIP EDGE

FASCIA

To reduce the quantity of water that might otherwise run off the rake end of a roof a length of beveled siding is often nailed in place along the rake. Some roofers position a rake of strip shingles along the rake edge to do the same thing.

Bring the roll of felt up and place it above the bundles. Take a lot of care doing this to make certain the felt will not roll down off the roof. If it does, it can easily kill whomever it may strike.

If you find the weight of a bundle too much to handle easily, break it in half and carry half a bundle at a time. Remember, it is a lot easier to go up the ladder twice with 50 pounds than to go up once with 100 pounds.

Laying the felt. Unroll enough felt to reach from one end of the roof to the other (rake edge to rake edge), plus 2 feet or so. The felt has two sides, one of which has lines; you want the lined side to face upward.

Go to either end of the felt. Adjust it so that it extends over the rake edge by about 6 inches and the lower edge of the felt at that point is flush with the eave. Drive a nail through the upper corner

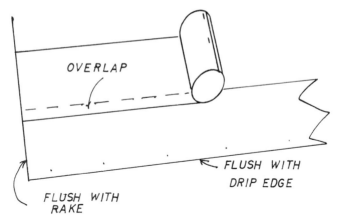

The 15-pound felt that goes atop a bare roof is laid as shown. Just a few short roofing nails are required.

of the felt, partway into the roof deck. This nail will prevent the felt from sliding down the roof at that point. Next, position yourself on the roof above the felt and walk away from the nail. As you do so, use your hand to smooth the felt and position it so that its lower edge is flush with the eave. In other words, you position the felt so that it is smooth and runs straight across the roof. As you do this, drive nails through the felt and partly into the roof. Position the nails about 3 feet apart and about 8 inches down from the top edge of the felt.

After you have crossed the roof this way, examine the felt. If it is still lying there nice and smooth, fine, If not, see what the cause is. You may have to remove some of the nails to remove the bumps. When the felt is lying perfectly smooth across the roof, its lower edge flush with the eave edge of the roof, go to this edge and nail the felt in place. Use one short roofing nail about every 3 feet positioned about 8 inches up from the eave. Now you can trim the felt that overhangs the rake edges; use two nails there, about 6 inches in, to hold the ends of the felt in place. Are all the nails in place, the felt smooth? Drive the nails snug. Do not drive the nailheads through the felt.

The succeeding strip of felt will overlap the in-place felt by 2 inches. Laying the second strip will do no harm, but it is not yet needed. Delay laying it until you actually need it. The less the felt is exposed to the sun, the less it will stretch and wrinkle in the heat. As soon as your shingles have come near to the 2-inch overlap, lay the next strip of felt down.

When you come to a hip ridge, run the felt up and over the ridge for a foot or so. Nail the end down. When you come to the main ridge, do the same. If the strips of felt work out to be just short of the ridge at both sides, lay another strip of felt lengthwise atop the ridge and nail its edges in place overlapping the two in-place strips.

Take the time necessary to keep the strips parallel with the eave edges of the roof. When the lines on the surface of the felt are positioned properly, they will help you lay your shingles in a straight line. In fact, experienced roofers use those lines and nothing more as guides.

EXPOSURE

The three-tab shingle is designed for an exposure of 5 inches. This exposure can be reduced to nothing by simply sliding the following shingle farther over the lower and in-place shingle. But the exposure cannot be stretched much beyond 6 inches because beyond this distance the mineral covering on the shingle stops and all that is visible is the black, tar-impregnated felt.

The exposure you select becomes important only when you approach the ridge. If the exposure you have selected is correct and accurately maintained, you will reach the ridge with one-fourth the width of a shingle projecting beyond. Then when you cap the ridge, the exposure of the last and highest course (row) of shingles will be the same as the exposure of the first and lowest, or beginning, course of shingles.

The way to do this is as follows: Measure the distance from the eave to the ridge and convert the number to inches. Then divide this number experimentally by either 5 or 6 or a fraction in between until you get a whole number as the answer. Say, for example, the eave-to-ridge distance is 26 feet 3 inches. Converting this to inches brings us to 315 inches. Dividing by 5¼ inches (after a great deal of figuring) brings us to 60. Thus, if we expose each shingle exactly 5¼ inches and lay 60 courses, we will hit the ridge just right.

The easier way is to fudge. Lay your shingles 5 inches to the weather (exposure) until you come within 3 feet or so of the ridge. Then stop nailing and lay down as many shingles as you need to, just one shingle above and atop the other with 5 inches of exposure, and see how you come out. If necessary, decrease the exposure of the remaining courses so that the shingles of the last course project over the ridge for 4 or 5 inches.

The reason for reducing rather than increasing the exposure of the last shingles is that they look better that way. There is a natural tendency for the exposure to look narrower as the eye approaches the ridge.

Starter width. The 12-inch-wide starter strip width, whether made of shingles or roll roofing, is fine for all latitudes up to about a line running westward from Washington, D.C. If your home is above that line and 5 or more miles in from the coast, it is best to use an 18-inch-wide starter strip, which perforce cannot be made of 12-inch-wide shingles but must be cut from a 90-pound, 36-inch-wide roll of mineralized roofing. (Some dealers carry 18-inch starters.) When your home is north of a line running westward from Boston or so, it is best to go to a 24-inch-wide starter strip. When north of Portland, Maine, or thereabouts, it is best to use a 36-inch-wide starter strip.

The reason for the starter strip is for protection against freeze-back. This is a roofer's term for frost that works its way back up beneath the shingles. The colder the average temperature, the farther up the roof these icy fingers reach. Since it is warmer under the roof than on the surface, the upper edge of this ice will melt from time to time and, being under the shingles, will leak into the house.

Installing the starter. Years ago it was common to install the starter and the first course of shingles with the lower edges projecting 1 or even 2 inches beyond the roof deck. It was assumed that the overhang helped keep the rainwater in the gutter. But not only is this overhang unsightly, it is also an aid to freezeback. The modern and much better method is to install a metal drip edge along the eave so that it projects 1 inch beyond the roof deck; then the starter strip and shingles are placed on top of it. The eave drip edge provides the projection that helps the rain find its way into the gutter. And since the drip edge is made of metal, the shingles cannot sag and become unsightly.

Some roofers also install drip edging along the rakes. Whereas

This is how shingles are cut and nailed to the rake end of a roof to produce a "straight-up" pattern, one slot above the other. Any type or width of starter may be used. Note that no nails are driven into the roof deck less than 3 inches from the edge.

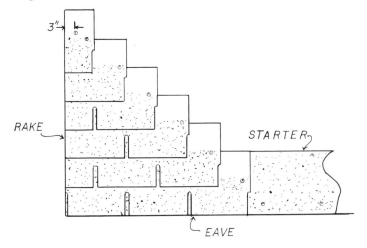

the eave edging is always spaced an inch or so clear of the deck, rake edging is usually positioned against the side of the building.

Eave edging is L-shaped and is generally 1 inch by 3 inches in width, 10 feet or more in length, with the wider side always placed on the roof. Eave edging is always installed first. Joints are made by simply overlapping the ends of the strips by a couple of inches, and one nail every 3 feet is plenty.

Rake edging, when used, is installed after the eave edging. The lower end of the rake edging overlaps the eave edging. The second and following strips of rake edging overlap the in-place edging by 1 or 2 inches. The top end of the rake edging is always cut 2 inches or so short of the ridge. Rake edging is usually 1½ by 2 to 3 inches wide. Generally the wider edge is nailed to the roof deck.

Always use aluminum drip edging and aluminum nails. The galvanized edging rusts in time, and then rust will drip down the side of the building. Some manufacturers offer rake edging in colors. Eave edging is not available in colors.

Returning to our job, start by installing a drip edge along the eave. Position it to project 1 inch beyond the roof deck. Nail the edge in place as suggested. Install rake edging if you want it. Now you are ready to lay down the starter.

If you are using shingles as a starter, place them mineral side up, slots facing uphill. Position the lower edge of the first and succeeding shingles flush with the lower edge of the drip edge. Place the end of the first shingle ¼ inch beyond the rake of the roof (or the rake edging if you are using it).

Nail the first starter shingle in place. Use four 1-inch nails. Place one nail 1 inch away from, but in line with, each slot. Then use two more nails in the same position near the half slots at the ends of the shingle. Do not drive the nails through the shingle less than 3 inches away from any roof edge. Butt the second starter shingle up against the first. Nail it in place and continue in this way across the width of the roof. Cut the next-to-last shingle so that the last shingle will project the required ¼ inch beyond the rake edge of the roof.

If you are using a strip of roll roofing for the starter, position it as suggested for the shingles. When using strip 12 inches wide, nail the upper edge in place with nails spaced 1 foot apart and 3 inches down from that edge. When the strip is 18 inches wide, use the same nail spacing about 6 inches down from the higher edge. When the strip is 24 inches wide, use the same spacing 4 inches down from the upper edge and make a second row 18 inches down. On a 36-inch-wide starter strip make the second row of nails about 1 foot up from the lower edge of the strip.

Again, if you are going to install a gutter that hangs from the roof deck, the gutter straps should be installed before you lay down the roof shingles.

Installing the shingles. At this point in the job you have nailed one layer of roofing felt across the lower edge of the roof, and you have also either nailed a starting strip of 90-pound mineralized roofing, mineral side up, across the bottom edge of the roof or installed a course of starter shingles atop the felt. The shingles, felt, and nails you will need are on the roof deck above you, out of the way but fairly close to where you will soon be working.

If you are right-handed you will probably find it easier if you start at the left side of the roof. If left-handed, working from right to left is probably easier. No matter; from either side the work is the same. Since most of us are right-handed, let us start our imaginary roof job at the lower left-hand corner of the roof.

Place a shingle, tabs pointing down, granular side up, flush with the left end of the starter course. This places the first shingle ¼ inch beyond the edge of the rake and flush with the end of the drip edge on the eave. As before, use four roofing nails to hold it in place. The nails go 1 inch higher than the slots and 1 inch from

A roofing job underway. Note that the entire roof has not been covered with felt.

the sides of the shingle, but no nail should be closer than 3 inches to the rake. Make the nails snug, but do not drive the heads into the shingle.

With one shingle in place, take a common nail, place it in line with the top edge of the first shingle and drive it partway into the deck. Then go to the other end of the roof and place another shingle there, exactly as you did the first. The lower edge of the shingle is placed flush with the edge of the drip edge on the eave and its end ¼ inch past the edge of the drip edge on the rake of the roof. However, do not nail the second shingle firmly in place. Just use two nails to position it temporarily.

Next, take a second common nail and drive it partway into the roof deck alongside the top edge of the second shingle. Now snap a chalk line between the two nails. Do this by attaching one end of the chalk line to one nail, wrapping the other end of the line around the second nail, and pulling the line taut. When the middle of the string is pulled up and released, the string snaps down against the roof and makes a clean, straight chalk line between the two nails. Now remove the two common nails and the temporary shingle at the far side of the roof. The holes left behind will cause no problem.

If you want all the tabs in alternate courses of shingles to be in a perfectly straight line above one another, you snap a perfectly vertical guideline parallel to the roof edge next to your first, in-place shingle. Use the end of this shingle and that of another shingle, temporarily positioned near the ridge of the roof, as a guide for the chalk line. The use of this line will be explained as we go along.

Now, you have one shingle permanently in place, with or without a vertical guideline. The next step is to lay the balance of the first course of shingles across the roof. This is done by placing the end of the second shingle against the first and nailing it in place, just like the first. Then continue placing and nailing shingles until you are just one shingle or part of a shingle short of the rake. Don't nail this shingle, just try it for fit.

If the last shingle just makes it—meaning its end overhangs the rake edge by the desired ¼ inch—fine, nail it in place. If the last shingle is too long, cut it. However, if cutting the last shingle to fit would make it less than 6 inches long, cut the next-to-last shingle as well as the last shingle so that the tab widths look right but the last shingle is more than 6 inches long. (You may have to pull up a nail to do this.)

You are now ready for the second course. Start at the same end as before, but instead of using a full shingle, cut one tab in the middle. Position this shingle on top and above the first shingle. Place its cut end flush with the other shingle and the desired ¼ inch beyond the rake end of the roof. Align its bottom edge a fraction of an inch above the slots. This will give you 5 inches of exposure. Vary it if you wish or need to. Now, before you nail this shingle, note that its slots appear directly above the center of the tabs in the shingle below. If you wish, snap another chalk line horizontally across the roof to help you keep the second course perfectly horizontal. Or wait until you are on the third or fourth

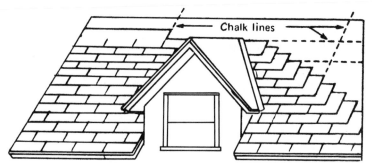

Use chalk lines as shown when you have to work on two sides and above a dormer. The lines will help keep the shingles lined up on both sides of the dormer. *Courtesy Asphalt Roofing Manufacturers Association.*

course. The roof will be just as water-tight if the lines are perfect as if they are not, and appearance will be improved. The second row of shingles is nailed down just like the first.

The third course begins with a shingle that is only two tabs wide. The fourth course begins with a shingle that is one and one-half tabs wide. The starting shingle of each course is reduced a half tab width until you start with half a tab, and then the next course up starts with another full shingle.

You can work your way all across the width of the roof one course at a time if you wish. However, experienced roofers generally work their way upward and across at the same time so that the leading edge of the shingles sort of forms an angle.

As you work your way upward along the rake, the single vertical line you snapped will help you keep the slots in line. As you work your way across, that line will be of no help. Again, if perfection is your game, snap more vertical lines as you work.

Patterns. When you start each course with shingles consecutively 6 inches smaller than the course below it, you will produce a vertical, or straight-up pattern. If you want the slits between the shingle tabs to move sideways as the viewer's eye ascends, start with the first shingle cut by 4 inches less than full width. Then cut the next-above shingle—the first of the succeeding course—by an additional 4 inches. When you get to the point where you would have to start the course with a 4-inch-wide shingle, make it 6 or 12 inches wide instead and cut the following shingle as necessary to accommodate it. Remember, no one can see the cuts between the shingles from the ground. As long as all the tab widths are identical, the roof will look perfect.

Cutting shingles. Turn the shingle to be cut upside down. Place a second shingle atop it. Slide the upper shingle to where its end marks the desired line of cut. Align the two shingles. The end of one shingle is now perfectly square across the other. Use this as a guide and score the lower shingle with your knife. Then break it off.

If you want the pattern to move to the right, cut the starting shingles on the left-hand side to the widths shown. *Courtesy Asphalt Roofing Manufacturers Association.*

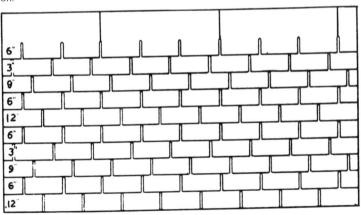

Incidentally, never try to work with shingles when the weather is so cold the shingle cannot be bent without breaking. If you must work in cold weather, keep the shingles inside and warm until you need them.

Ridges and valleys. Let us hope you haven't encountered any so far because they are not discussed until Chapter 14.

To cut a shingle straight across without troubling to use a square, place one shingle atop the other as a guide. Always cut into a shingle from the back side, as shown; otherwise the knife wears down even more rapidly than it usually does.

13

Shingling Over an Old Roof

The type and amount of work and material necessary to prepare an old roof for a covering of new asphalt shingles depends on the nature and condition of the roof and your concern with its finished appearance. If it is a workshed roof out back somewhere and all you want to do is to make it watertight, that is one matter. If it is the roof on your home, that is another matter.

WOOD SHINGLE ROOFS

No matter what condition the shingles are in, the first step to reroofing with asphalt shingles is to remove the ridge shingles. If there is a metal cap on the ridge of the type that sits atop the shingles try to remove it without damaging it. You can use it again. You will find a "cat's paw"—a tool made for pulling out nails—very useful for this. Other metal ridgecap designs are usually difficult to use with asphalt shingles, and you usually can be more certain of a watertight joint here if you remove the cap. In any event, look it over carefully before you destroy it. If you reinstall it, be sure to use nails of the same metal as the cap.

Next, inspect the wood shingles. If they are in fair to good condition, you can let them be and provide a smooth deck by nailing feathering strips—wedge-shaped pieces of wood—below the butt ends of the wood shingles. As an alternative, you can cover the old shingles with sheets of ⅜-inch inexpensive plywood. Stagger the joints and use 10-penny common nails driven into the rafters.

In both cases, cut the old wood shingles back to the rake trim and the fascia at the eaves. Install rake edging to hide the edges of the old shingles and plywood or feathering. And, as usual, install drip edging along the eaves, as described in Chapter 12. When using plywood, cut it about 1 inch short of the ridge. You don't want a sharp edge there.

Another approach is to remove all the old wood shingles and not fool with plywood or feathering strips. If the roof deck is solid beneath the shingles, no problem. You can lay the new shingles directly on top. If there is no deck in the usual sense, but just a number of spaced sheathing boards, you can either fill the spaces between the old boards with new boards of equal thickness and roof over the deck you have made, or you can cover the spaced sheathing with sheets of plywood. In the latter it is best to go to ½-inch thick panels.

If the spaced sheathing boards are less than 1 inch thick, or if they are in bad condition, do not fill the spaces between them with more wood nor cover them with plywood. Instead, remove them all and redeck the roof, using 1-inch roofers or ½-inch plywood.

Use a pinch bar, small crowbar, claw hammer, and/or a shovel to help you remove the old shingles and boards. Pull all nails. If you can't remove them, pound them flush with the surface of the rafters.

ASPHALT SHINGLE ROOFS

Examine the old roof carefully. Determine if there is more than one layer of old shingles on the roof and decide whether or not the surface of the old shingles is satisfactorily smooth.

When the old shingles are badly curled or there are too many layers of old shingles on the roof, remove all the shingles and felt. Roof deck holes more than an inch or so across must be repaired. *Courtesy Asphalt Roofing Manufacturers Association.*

If there are two or more layers of shingles on the roof, check with the building department as to whether or not your roof can carry the additional load. Remember a 64- to 40-foot roof, for example, requires some 7,200 pounds of asphalt shingles to cover it. If there are already two prior roofs, the third roof will result in a total shingle load of possibly 21,600 pounds—or nearly 11 tons.

If there is only one layer or if there are two layers but the surface is bumpy and lumpy, be advised that there is no practical way of laying new shingles atop the old and producing an attractive and smooth job. The only practical solution is to strip the roof down to its deck—remove all the old shingles. When you do this, make certain you remove all the nails and all the splinters your work may provoke. Then sweep the roof clean.

At this point, for all practical purposes you have a new roof deck; so proceed exactly as described in Chapter 12.

Let us assume, however, that you have either one or two layers

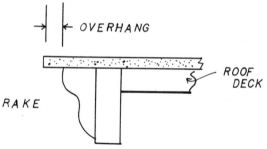

The edge of your shingles should overhang the rake edge of your roof by no more than about ¼ inch.

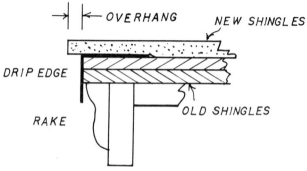

When reroofing, cut the old shingles back to the rake edge trim or moulding as it is sometimes called. Install an aluminum drip edge to hide the old shingle edges and then apply the new shingles.

of old roofing that are satisfactorily smooth, and that the roof is fully capable of carrying the additional load you propose. To lay a new roof atop this old one, start by carefully removing all the ridge capping. Take care not to injure the shingles you plan to leave in place. Use your knife and carefully cut the side edges of the roofing back to the rake trim. Then cut the bottom edges of the old roofing back to the roof deck. Here you have a choice. You can install drip edging if you wish, or not. If you don't mind the sight of the thick edges of two or three layers of shingles poking over the rake, forget the edging. If the sight is objectionable, install it.

Sweep the old roof clean. Do not lay down any felt. You will secure better results without it. The procedure from here on to completion is almost exactly the same as if you were working on a clean deck. The difference is this: Whereas on a new or clean deck you would begin shingling with a 12-inch-wide starter course, on "old" work you cut the starter shingles by 7 inches. Or, if you are using a strip, cut it by the same amount. Thus the width of the starter is only 5 inches.

Next, when you position the first shingle (and all the rest), take care to see that the top edge of that shingle does not rest atop the next higher shingle but butts up against its bottom edge. In this way you avoid making bumps where two and three thicknesses of shingles would otherwise be atop one another.

When applying new shingles over old, the width of the first course of shingles or starting strip should be no wider than the exposure of the first course of in-place shingles.

The shingles following the first course are full width and are positioned tabs pointing down and flush with the eave edge of the old shingles, or the drip edge.

Next, the shingles are laid up and nailed in place as usual. The black spots on top of the shingles are spots of cement which help seal the next course of shingles in place.

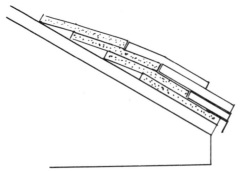

An exaggerated side view of the first or eave courses on a proper reroofing job. Note how the narrow shingle enables all the following shingles to lie reasonably flat.

That is all the difference there is between laying shingles on a clear roof deck and laying them atop old shingles. However, the position of the old shingles more or less holds you to the same exposure. This can be helpful and you can use the old shingles as a guide for laying the new when the old shingles are straight. When they are not, try cutting off some of the back edge of the new shingle to permit you to move it a little.

OTHER OLD ROOFS

We have discussed reroofing existing wood shingle or shake roofs and existing three-tab strip shingle roofs. There are, as mentioned in Chapter 10, a number of other types of asphalt shingles in use. They include Dutch lap, T-lock, giant individual American, individual hex shingles, three-tab hex shingles, and others. In most cases it is impossible to secure a smooth roof when laying three-tab strip shingles over anything else but three-tab strip or wood shingles.

So if your roof has any of these other shingles and you want an attractive roof, the old shingles have to be removed.

14

Ridges and Valleys

CAPPING A RIDGE

New work. One side of the roof is covered at a time. If the *mineralized* portion of the topmost course of shingles just reaches the peak, perfect. Nail the top course down. Fold the black, or unmineralized, portion of the shingles over the ridge and use a few nails to hold the ends down. If the mineralized portion of the top course of shingles misses the peak by no more than 2 inches, that isn't perfect, but it is acceptable. Nail the shingles down, fold the black edges over, and nail them down. However, if the top course misses by more than 2 or so inches, it is best to install an additional course of shingles.

That takes care of one side of the roof. The adjoining side of the roof is shingled the same way as the first. The shingles on the top course of the second side of the roof are nailed down over the shingle ends that have been folded over the ridge from the first side. The top edges of the top course on the second side are then folded over the ridge. However, if necessary, the ends of these shingles are cut back so that they do not project more than 2 inches past the ridge.

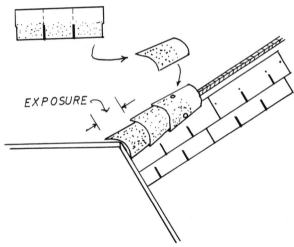

EXPOSURE

How strip shingles are cut into three pieces and used to cap a ridge. Generally ridge capping is started at both ends of the ridge. The last cap is positioned somewhere in the middle. Many roofers cut the cap tabs at an angle so that the hidden portion is narrower than the exposed portion. This makes for a somewhat neater job.

This done, you are ready to cap the ridge. Start by cutting as many standard three-tab strip shingles into however many capping shingles you may need. Each strip shingle becomes three capping shingles. Cut along the two tabs cuts. Ascend to the ridge. Face the rake end. Bend a capping shingle to conform to the pitch of the roof. Place its normally lower, granulated edge crosswise in line with the other shingles' edging on the roof. In other words, the end of the capping shingle will extend beyond the roof by ¼ inch. Nail the first capping shingle in place using two roofing nails. Place them to either side, 1 inch in from the edges of the shingle and 6 inches in from its end. Place a second capping shingle atop the first. Bend it to conform to the roof pitch. Permit 5 inches of the first capping shingle to be exposed. Nail the second in place, partially atop the first. Position the two nails just as before. Continue on this way until you have covered the entire ridge and have come

A few examples of ridge capping. *Courtesy Asphalt Roofing Manufacturers Association.*

to the other end. Adjust the exposure of the last few shingles so that the very last is 2 or 3 inches short of the end of the roof.

You now have capped the entire ridge. The only problem is that you have a strip of black—the end of a shingle—showing. To cover this, take a capping shingle and cut it short by several inches. You now have a shingle without any black showing. Position it atop the ridge, one end flush with the other shingles lining the rake end of the roof. Nail this last capping shingle in place with four nails. Cover each nailhead with a daub of roofing cement.

Old work. Carefully remove all the old ridge capping along with the nails. Proceed exactly as previously discussed. Just make certain your nails are long enough to really bite into the roof deck.

If you have removed intact a metal ridgecap, place it atop the ridge, overlapping the shingles underneath, and nail it in place. Then seal each nail with a daub of roofing cement.

Capping a hip roof. Shingle the entire roof first. When and where you have shingles that overlap the hip ridge, cut them flush with the ridge. Then start at the bottom end of the hip. Cut the lower end of the first shingle to conform to the angle of the two eaves. Let the first shingle overhang the roof deck as much as the other shingles underneath. Work your way up the hip ridge until you come to the main ridge. Finish all hip ridges first. The main ridge capping shingles go over the ends of the hip ridges.

LINING VALLEYS

A valley is a concave junction of two roof sections. When the two roof sections have the same pitch and are more or less the

Hip ridges are capped after the main ridge is capped, starting with the lower end of the hip, as indicated.

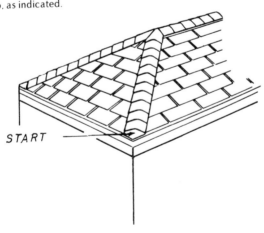

START

same size from eave to ridge, there is usually little problem at the valley. Rain coming sideways down the roof surfaces joins in the valley and flows straight down to the gutter. When one roof section has a much steeper pitch or is considerably larger, more water and water at a faster rate enters the valley from the steeper, larger roof section and tends to flow *across* the valley and under the adjacent shingles of the more gently sloping, smaller section.

There are a number of ways of lining a valley and a number of ways of treating straight valleys between equal surfaces, straight valleys between unequal surfaces, valleys with turns, and blind valleys. The following suggested methods are the simplest. If care is taken, they will work just as well as the others.

Materials. You can use metal to line the valleys or you can use 90-pound mineralized felt. The metal looks better, especially the copper, and lasts longer, but since the 90-pound felt will last just as long as the shingles and it costs but a fraction of the price of the metal, most homeowners opt for the thick felt. The use of the thick felt is discussed in the following sections. The use of metal is covered at the end of this chapter.

Smooth valleys. The following method is used when the valley has no turns and bends and when the pitch and size of the two roof sections that join to form the valley are more or less alike, meaning that just as much rainwater will be running down into the valley from one as from the other.

Like all valley work, you must begin while you still have several feet of unshingled roof space on both sides of the valley. If you are covering a new roof or a stripped old roof, there will be nothing between the new shingles and the valley except the 15-pound felt you just laid down. If you are covering an old roof, there will be nothing between the new shingles and the valley except the old, in-place shingles.

If there is an old valley lining and it is in fair to good condition, let it be, but make certain all the nails are driven home. If the old valley is torn or ripped just a little, seal the holes with plastic cement. If it is badly ripped, remove all of it. Then be certain to sweep the entire area clean.

Secure a roll of the 90-pound felt with a color matching that of your shingles. Each roll is 34 feet long, 3 feet wide, and weighs 90 pounds. Measure the length of the valley. Add 1 foot to this dimension, then cut that length from the roll. Stretch this piece out, granular side down. Cut it into two strips—one, 1 foot wide; the other, 2 feet wide.

Position the narrow strip, mineralized side down, in the valley. Let the bottom end extend 1 inch beyond the eave. Let the balance of the strip extend above and beyond the top end of the valley. Later you will cut this end of the narrow strip—and the wide strip that goes on top of it—back so that it is covered by no more than

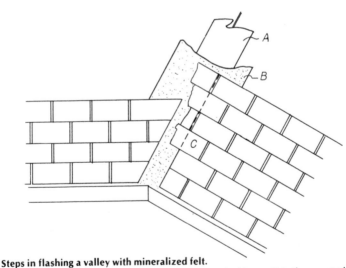

Steps in flashing a valley with mineralized felt.
A. The 1-foot wide strip is nailed in place smooth side up. It is then coated with roofing cement.
B. The 2-foot wide strip is nailed in place, mineral side up.
C. The shingles are laid up as usual. Their ends are then cut to the line, as shown.

two courses (rows) of shingles or by the cap shingles that go on a ridge.

Returning to the 1-foot-wide strip positioned lengthwise in the valley: Nail one edge down. Position the nails about 1 foot apart and about 1 inch in from the edge of the felt. Now, force the strip as deeply into the valley as it will go; at the same time nail the other side down as you go.

Next, coat the entire 1-foot-wide strip with a ⅛-inch-thick layer of plastic roofing cement. *Do not use tar*. When applying, use a worn glove or a small trowel. Next, center the wider strip of felt, granular side up, atop the in-place strip. Press it firmly down into the cement. Take care to make certain there are no folds or bubbles. Fasten the wide strip in place with nails 1 inch in from the edges and 1 foot apart.

Now the valley is lined with the lining sticking up about 11 inches beyond the upper end of the valley. Let it be for the moment. Return to laying shingles on the roof. Stop when the shingles reach to within an inch or so of *the center* of the valley. Do not drive nails through any shingle that will also penetrate farther than 1 or 2 inches from the edge of the valley lining. Let that portion of the shingle just lie there for the present.

When your shingles reach the top of the valley, try to bend the top end of the valley lining back so that it lies flat on the roof. You may or may not be able to do this, depending on the configuration of the roof. In any event, do not let a lump form here, but cut the strip back as far as you have to. Then place your shingles or caps over the end of the valley lining so that rain coming down the shingle will enter the valley. If you do not have more than 5 inches of shingle overlaying the valley, cement the underside of the shingle to the top of the valley lining. This is done to prevent the wind from driving water up and under the shingles at this point.

Next you need to trim the ends of the shingles that overlap the valley. To secure a good-looking job, use a chalk line to guide you while you cut. If you cannot find a helper to hold one end of the line, weight it and hang the weighted end over the ridge of the roof. Snap two parallel lines about 2½ to 3 inches apart to each side of the center of the valley. Then cut along the chalk lines. To reduce the chance of your cutting into the felt, place a board under your knife as you go.

The shingle ends cut, return to the top of the valley and work your way down, lifting each shingle end as you do so. Whenever you uncover a sharp-ended shingle pointing into the valley, cut its end off. *Cut the underlying shingle points, not the tips of the shingles that are on top.* Now trim the lower end of the valley lining flush with the adjoining shingles.

Next, return to the cut-and-trimmed shingles. Some of them will only have a few nails holding them. These shingles require additional nails. Lift the overlapping shingles as necessary and drive the needed nails in, but do not drive any nails into the deck that will also go through the double thickness of valley felt. In other words, keep your nails 9 inches or so from the center of the valley.

If the roof's pitch is low and your area is subject to driving rain, you can reduce the chance of water getting beneath the cut shingle ends by cementing them down with a little plastic roofing cement. Do not use a lot, since heat may cause the cement to run down and discolor the valley.

Valleys between roofs of unequal pitch or size. The procedure is the same, with a small exception. Study the two roofs where they meet at the valley and determine how the water will run in a heavy rain. It will of course run from the higher or steeper roof across the valley and up onto the lower, smaller roof. Install the valley lining as before. However, when shingling the lower and possibly smaller roof, the roof onto which the water will run, stop nailing when you reach the 90-pound felt. Instead of nailing these shingle ends down, cement them down. In other words, instead of just placing a daub of cement near the end of the cut shingles, use a little more, but don't use so much that the cement runs down and slops up the job. Bear in mind that you don't have to do this with all the shingles on that side of the valley. The use of cement in place of nails is only necessary where water may leave the valley and run up on the roof.

Blind valleys. In some roof designs there are two valleys that join to form a third valley, called a blind valley. The potential problem here is that the flow of water down the two higher valleys meets in opposing directions and can pile up at that point. This leads to a side movement of the water, which can get beneath the adjacent shingles. The same solution can be used here. However, instead of merely cementing down the shingles on the lower side of the valley, you should cement down the shingles in an area 2 or more feet across, centered on the junction of the three valleys.

Lining bent valleys. Bent valleys, valleys that make a turn in their run down to the gutter, can also be lined with 90-pound felt, as previously suggested.

Start by positioning and nailing the narrower of the two strips to the lower portion of the valley. Then position and nail the narrow upper strip. Cut the upper strip so that its lower end butts against the lower, in-place strip. Now apply the cement as before and position and nail the 2-foot-wide strip over the lower portion of the valley—the portion below the bend. Then do the same with the upper portion, but this time, instead of butting its end, let the end overlap the in-place strip and cement the joint.

Next, when you shingle up to the valley, cement down the ends of the shingles that rest on the valley strip for a distance of a foot or more above and below the bend and on both sides of the valley.

Low-pitched valleys. When the pitch of the valley is less than 5 inches in 12 it is best to make the first strip of felt 18 inches wide and the second strip 36 inches wide.

Northern valleys. When the building is at a latitude north of Boston or thereabouts it is best to make the first strip 18 inches wide and the second strip 36 inches wide.

Fully laced valleys. There is another way of lining valleys. This method provides more positive insurance against leakage, although the finished appearance is never as neat as that of a smoothly lined valley, and in some instances it is more difficult and even impractical to use.

The best way to describe the installation of a laced valley may be by indirection. Assume you are a dedicated roofer who doesn't know the meaning of the word *quit*. You begin laying shingles at the eave of one roof section. When you come to the valley that separates the first roof section from the second, you do not stop

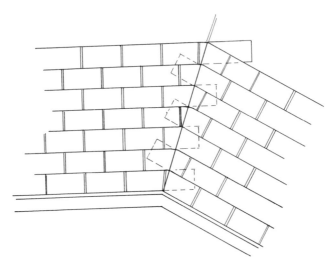

Interlacing of the roof shingles at the junction of two roof sections is accomplished by overlapping the shingles where they meet. The uppermost shingles are cut along a straight line down the center of the valley.

but continue right across. You repeat this sincere performance with the second and following courses until you have shingled both roof sections up to their ridges. Or, phrased another way, to lace a valley you simply shingle right on over it.

This is easier said than done, but is not very difficult if you accept the fact that you will have to fudge when you go from a low-pitched to a high-pitched roof section. The only sure way for a beginner to lace a valley is to lay the shingles down without nailing them and see how they look. Sometimes you have to "lose a beat," meaning you have to drop a tab on a shingle or start in mid tab. Sometimes you have to work in another and additional course of shingles on the higher roof.

When the change in pitch and direction from one roof to the next is great, you have to overlap the ends of alternate courses of shingles as they cross the valley. Following, the ends of the upper courses of shingles are cut to a straight line directly above the center of the valley.

A completed, laced valley. Look carefully and you will see that all the shingles are not in line as they cross the valley, but the end result is pleasing. *Courtesy Asphalt Roofing Manufacturers Association.*

Lining valleys with metal. In this writer's opinion, the only two metals practical for valley lining are aluminum and copper, 20 gauge or thicker. Galvanized steel always rusts with time, and the rust can run down and stain the building. Copper on paper—or metalized paper, if you will—should not be used alone. It is much too thin even in the 3-ounce thickness.

The usual method of applying metal valley lining is to lay the metal directly in the gutter atop 15-pound roofing felt. Generally the metal strip is 14 or more inches wide and is nailed down every 6 inches, with the nails about ½ inch in from the edge. The nails must be of the same metal as the liner or holes will form in the metal in short order. Following this installation, the shingles are laid up as previously described.

This writer advocates a different method. Start with 90-pound felt, at least 2 feet wide. Nail it in place, mineral side up. Then nail the metal in place after giving its bottom edges a thin coat of plastic roofing cement. The area of water protection is much wider, and there is less chance of water getting under the metal. The plastic seals the nail holes.

To secure lasting results from metallized paper, line the valley with two layers of 90-pound mineralized felt. Then cement the underside of the paper to the valley and use a few nails along its edges. Seal the nailheads with cement. This method provides the appearance of metal at low cost along with the protection of the two layers of 90-pound felt.

15

Flashing

Wherever the surface of a roof meets a vertical surface, such as a chimney or a dormer wall, the joint must be flashed. The reason is that while plastic cement will seal the joint, time and the inter-movement of wall and roof will open it. Flashing does not provide a joint; instead it bridges the opening. Like a shingled roof, which in itself is not watertight but keeps the building dry by directing water over the joints, flashing directs the flow of water away and over the joint between roof and wall or chimney.

FLASHING A ROOF AND VERTICAL SURFACE

This is most easily accomplished before the siding, whatever it may be, has been installed. Start by shingling the roof in the usual manner, but leave about ¾ inch of space between the edge of the shingles and the side of the wall. Next take a number of 5- or 6- by 6-inch squares of 18-gauge aluminum and bend them in half at an angle. The angle should be such that when the bent square is placed on the roof, one-half points straight up. In other words, the angle of the bend conforms to the pitch of the roof. Now go to the lowest junction between the wall and the roof. Place one side

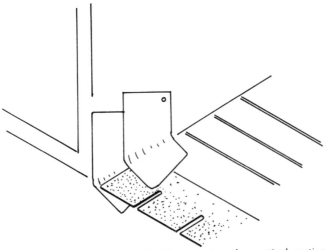

Basic arrangement of parts when flashing a roof and a vertical portion of a building. The lowest piece of flashing is nailed in place first. Then a shingle is laid atop the flashing. The second piece of step flashing is nailed in place and followed by the second shingle. This procedure is continued for the entire junction between the wall and roof.

of the bent aluminum square against the wall and slip the other portion up and under the uppermost shingle—at that point. Press the bent metal as deeply into the corner of the wall as it will easily go. Drive a roofing nail through the top upper corner of the metal, into the wall. Now, move up one shingle and slip a second bent square over that shingle and also over the nailed-on metal square. Repeat this procedure until you come to the end of the wall. This is called step flashing. If you look upward, you will see open spaces beneath the flashing. This is normal. But since water usually runs downhill, the water will not get under the flashing and into your home.

Where siding is already in place, you have to remove some of the nails so that you can slip the flashing into place. It is the same arrangement, just more difficult to do.

When and where the old flashing is solid, you can cut it close to the surface of the roof and slip the new flashing up under its edge. Use plastic cement or a high-grade caulking, such as butyl rubber sealant, to hold the flashing in place. In either case, apply a generous quantity and, after the cement or sealent has dried for a few days, give it several coats of aluminum paint. That will extend its life.

FLASHING CHIMNEYS

Flashing a chimney may involve one or two types of flashing. When the chimney is alongside the rake edge of the roof, step flashing is used. When it is within the roof, step flashing plus flat flashing, with or without a cricket, may be used.

Chimneys are step-flashed exactly like walls. The only difference is that the top edge of the flashing has to be bent into a horizontal position so that it can be slipped into openings left in the chimney by the mason. When the chimney has no slots, or the slots are filled with old flashing, you can provide slots by either carefully chiseling the old flashing free or making new slots with a power-driven carborundum-blade saw. Make the slots about ¾ inch deep and no wider than necessary to accept the metal, and step the slots so that the flashing can follow the shingles.

When the chimney springs up somewhere near the ridge, the sides of the chimney are flashed with step flashing, but the front and back sides of the chimney have to be sealed with what may be termed flat flashing.

On a new chimney a horizontal slot some 6 to 8 inches above the roof deck will be left open on both the upper and lower sides of the chimney. A sheet of metal, preferably 18-gauge aluminum (copper, if you don't mind the expense, is even better), is cut 10 inches longer than the width of the chimney and about 1 foot wide. First a ¾-inch-wide right angle bend is made along one side. This "lip" is to enter the slot on the lower side of the chimney. Then the sheet is bent to something less than 90 degrees along its middle. The angle and position of this bend is such that when the lip enters

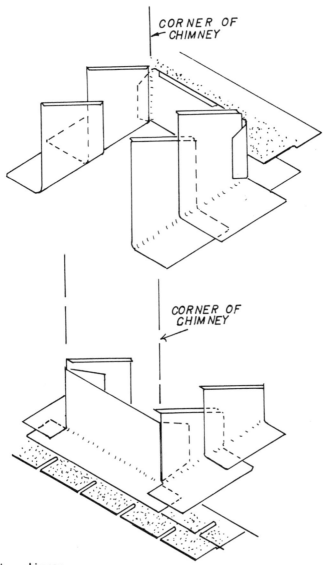

CORNER OF CHIMNEY

CORNER OF CHIMNEY

Flashing a chimney.
A. How the upper portion of the chimney (not shown) may be flashed. Flat flashing is used in front, step flashing on the sides. Front corners must be sealed by cementing or soldering (if you use copper).
B. How the lower half of a chimney may be flashed. Note that flat flashing goes on top of following roof shingles.

the slot, the lower portion of the metal will rest smoothly *atop* the shingles below the chimney.

Next, place the flashing against the lower side of the chimney, slip the lip in the slot, and see how everything fits. You want the middle bend to sit right down against the top edges of the shingles. Now, let us assume that the width of the chimney is exactly 24 inches and that the length of the sheet of metal is exactly 34 inches. Cut a slit along each side of the middle bend for a distance of exactly 5 inches. Cut the lips off above this point on both sides. Cut the lower half of the metal—the portion below the two slits—off. This leaves you with two 5-inch-long tabs on both sides. Bend them back. Now slip the bent and cut piece of metal against the lower side of the chimney, lip in the slot, tabs against the sides of the chimney. If it fits snugly, nail the bottom section atop the shingles. Use just two nails near the corners. Seal the nail heads with a daub of cement. Seal the lip inside the chimney with mortar or caulking.

Next, install step flashing on both sides of the chimney. Let the flashing extend below the ends of the flat flashing. If you have any doubt as to whether or not the water will be carried past the ends of the flat flashing, seal the opening.

Now we have to flash the upper horizontal portion of the chimney. Make a second piece of flat flashing exactly like the first. However, the tabs of this flashing go above the step flashing, and the upper edge of the flashing goes below the next-above shingle. At this point, if you look carefully, you have two openings in the flashing facing uphill. These openings have to be closed. The best way to do this is with preformed corners. If you can purchase them to fit, coat the corner and nearby shingle area with plastic cement, press the corner in place, and put two nails through the upper edges of each corner. Seal with a daub of cement and lower the shingles over them. If you cannot secure preformed corners to fit, seal the openings with a generous quantity of plastic cement.

If the old flashing on the chimney is in good condition, try to loosen the nails and get the new shingles properly positioned. If you can't do that, cut the old flashing near the roof and slip the edges of the new flashing underneath.

Years ago, when copper had a reasonable price, chimney flashing was made by soldering closed the joints we are concerned with. Today, we use plastic cement to seal the openings. Aluminum can be soldered, but it cannot easily be done on a roof.

Crickets. When the chimney is near the top of the roof, the previously suggested method for flashing is fine because there isn't a huge buildup of water against the upper side of the chimney. When the chimney is near the bottom of the roof, it is wise to install a cricket if there isn't one already.

A cricket is a small ridged roof that rests between the upper side of the chimney and the roof itself. It diverts water away from the chimney.

If there is a cricket, let it be. The shingles above and to the side of the cricket rest on the cricket so there is no need to move it if you are reroofing. If the cricket metal is rusted, coat it with plastic cement. That will hold it for another twenty-five years.

If it is a new house, construct a cricket out of wood and cover it with metal. Or, make the entire cricket from metal. Use 16-gauge or heavier aluminum. Most sheet metal shops will construct one to your specifications.

FLASHING PIPE

Every building has two or more pipes coming up through the roof. One is the main stack, and the other is a vent. Before you start to roof, purchase two preformed metal flashings that fit the pipe sizes involved. Slip the flashing over the pipe as you lay shingles. The upper (higher) edge of the flashing goes beneath the higher (on the roof) shingles. The lower edge of the flashing goes on top of the shingles. Two nails through the high side of the metal, the side that is covered by shingles, will hold it in place. Seal the joint between the pipe and the flashing with cement.

16

Roll Roofing

Roll roofing is used as an underlay for asphalt shingles and as the exposed surface on a roof. Exposed roll roofing is used on barns, garages, storage sheds, and small commercial buildings having roof pitches ranging downward to as low as 2/12. Roll roofing provides as watertight and as permanent a roof covering as individual asphalt shingles. It is much easier and faster to apply and costs considerably less. However, at its very best, roll roofing is not pleasing in appearance. Therefore it is almost never used on a private home where it can be seen from the ground. Its life expectancy is nothing to brag about either. Generally, you can count on roll roofing for no more than ten years, and no matter what type or brand you buy, roll roofing carries no warranty.

AVAILABLE MATERIAL

Roll roofing, sometimes called saturated felt, is most often manufactured in weights of 15 to 120 pounds per exposed square, in rolls 36 inches wide. The heavier the weight of the roll, the thicker the material and the greater its life expectancy when exposed to the elements.

In addition to different weights, roll roofing is available either smooth or granulated. The smooth has no crushed stone on its surface. The granulated has. The smooth rolls are made for underlaying shingles and for constructing built-up roofing, which consists of layers of smooth felt completely cemented to one another to form one solid waterproof layer. It is used for roofs having a pitch of less than 2/12. The granulated sheeting is made for direct exposure.

Another type of roll is mineralized for half its width. The other half is smooth. This type of roll material is usually called double exposure stock; sometimes it is referred to as half-coated stock. It is designed for a 17-inch exposure with a 19-inch overlap. Like the other roll sheeting, it is also 36 inches wide.

Patterned-edge roll is similar to the mineralized roll material with the exception of one edge. The edge is cut into a pattern. Whereas the standard mineralized roll sheet lays down with a straight edge, the patterned-edge roll lays down with a patterned edge that somewhat resembles shingles. This material comes 36 inches wide, but breaks into two rolls, each half that width. The usual width of exposure is 7 to 8 inches for each half.

The last of the more or less commonly used roll roofing types is called Traffic-Top or Rough-Top. It runs about 200 pounds to the square and is very heavily mineralized. It is designed to be walked on. It is used on apartment house roofs and exposed porch roofs. It is seldom used on a new home.

Originally, old porch roofs that could be reached directly from a second-story door were covered with canvas impregnated with white lead. Not only was this troublesome and expensive, it was poisonous. Present-day walk-on roofing is simply cemented directly in place on the old, cleaned-off roof deck. As few nails as possible are used to hold it in place. Nailheads are sealed with silicone cement.

Where used. To summarize:

15-pound felt is used dry beneath all shingles placed on an otherwise bare deck.

15-pound felt is cemented and doubled and used beneath shingles on roofs having a pitch of less than 4/12 but more than 2/12.

30-pound smooth felt is used mainly for built-up roofing.

90-pound mineralized felt is used for exposed roofing down to pitches of 2/12, starter strips, valley linings, and ridge covering or capping.

Double exposure felt is used for exposed roofing with pitches down to 2/12.

Patterned edge roofing is used for exposed roofing with pitches down to 4/12.

200-pound mineralized felt is used for exposed roofing that will be walked on.

UNDERLAYING SHINGLES

When you want to lay strip shingles—or any other type of individual shingles—or patterned-edge roll sheets on a roof that has a pitch of 4/12 to a minimum of 2/12, it is necessary to seal the roof beneath the shingles to make certain it will not leak in a high wind. (Wind can drive rain up and under nearly flat shingles.)

Start by laying down a 19-inch-wide (or wider) strip of 15-pound felt as a starter strip. Make the felt smooth and use just a few nails to hold it in place. Use a notched-edge trowel to cover the entire surface of the starter strip with a layer of plastic asphalt cement. Lay the cement down at the approximate rate of 2 gallons per 100 square feet of felt.

Lay a second started strip consisting of the full width (36 inches) of a 15-pound roll of felt atop the first starter strip. Press the second strip firmly against the first. You now have a 36-inch-wide starter strip running across the bottom edge of your roof. Use a few nails to hold it in place.

Next, spread another layer of cement along the length of the felt but confined to the upper 19 inches. Press a third sheet of 15-pound felt atop the second sheet so that it just covers the 19-inch-wide layer of cement. Use a few nails to hold the third sheet in place. Repeat the process until you reach the ridge. In effect, you are covering your roof with 15-pound felt with a cemented-in-place overlap of 19 inches.

Next, drip edges are nailed in place. Following, the shingles are nailed on in the usual way. However, you must use self-sealing shingles (with factory-applied adhesive beneath each shingle tab) or you must daub a little cement beneath each tab yourself. Also, you should allow no more than 4 inches of exposure.

APPLYING 90-POUND ROOFING

Exposed-nail technique. Lay one full-width sheet across the lower edge of the roof as a starter sheet. Position and trim the sheet as you would the starter strip for shingle roofing. Start at either rake end. Nail that end to the roof with nails 2 inches in from the edge and about 2 to 3 inches apart. Go to the farther end of the sheet. Pull it taut across the roof. Drive the necessary nails to hold it down. Go to the lower edge of the sheet. Nail it in place, take care to stagger the nails—if you put them in a straight line, you may split the deck timber—and also take care not to pull or push on the sheet and thereby produce lumps along its length.

Place a second full-width sheet of the 90-pound roll roofing across the roof deck. Make it overlap the in-place sheet by at least 3 inches. More will do no harm. Nail it in place. If you want a more watertight job, spread a little cement along the top 2 inches of in-place sheeting before you nail the overlap down. If you want a somewhat better-looking job, measure the eave-to-ridge distance

A

Steps in applying roll roofing.
  A. A layer of 15-pound felt has been laid down and the roll roofing has been laid
     atop it. Here, the selvage edge of the roll roofing is being nailed in place.
     (About twice as many nails as necessary are being used.)
  B. The second course or layer of roll roofing is being positioned. Note the
     overlap.

B

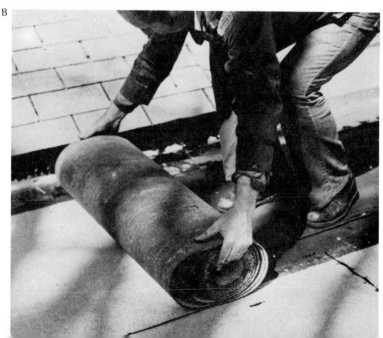

C

C. The edge of the roofing is lifted up and a little tar or roofing cement is applied.

D. Roofing cement is also applied to the ends of the roofing felt.

D

and divide it evenly by the number of sheets that you plan to use. In this way you will be able to plan the overlaps so that you can make them fairly equal and thus improve the overall appearance of the roof.

Concealed-nail technique. Start by nailing a 9-inch-wide or wider starter strip along the bottom of the roof. Space the nails about 4 inches apart and 1 or 2 inches in from the edge. Nail all four sides of the starter strip. Nail identical strips of 90-pound felt to the rake sides of the roof. Cover the bottom strip with a generous, smooth layer of plastic roofing cement. Cover the side strips with a similar layer to a distance of about 4 feet up from the bottom of the roof.

Place a full-width sheet of 90-pound felt across the bottom of the roof. Press it firmly and smoothly down on the starting strip along the eave and the strips along the rakes. Nail the upper edge of the full sheet in place with nails about 4 inches apart and 1 to 2 inches down from the edge. Coat the top 6 inches of this now in-place sheet with plastic cement. Apply more plastic cement to the side strips. Lay a second full-width sheet of the felt across the roof, overlapping the in-place sheet by the correct distance, and press it firmly in place. Nail its top edge down as before. Continue cementing, nailing, and spreading the sheeting until you reach the ridge. Ridge treatment is covered a bit further along.

APPLYING DOUBLE-COVERAGE ROOFING

Either of the two procedures just explained can be used. If you don't mind the nails, just nail away. If you want the tightest of all possible jobs, coat the entire 19 inches of selvage with cement. If not, just coat the top 6 inches with cement. Just remember when you are planning to use this material that you cover a strip only 17 inches wide with each 36-inch-wide strip or sheet of material as it comes from the roll.

CAPPING THE RIDGE

The same method discussed in capping ridges with individual shingles is used to cap ridges on roofs covered with any of the roll roofings just discussed. However, instead of 1- by 1-foot caps, we use 1- by 3-foot caps that can be cut out of the roll roofing or, more easily, out of a 1-foot-wide starter roll.

To product an attractive or at least a neat-looking job, snap two chalk lines 6 inches on either side of the ridge. Make certain the lines are parallel with the peak of the ridge. These lines will guide you when you cap the ridge.

Start at the low end if you are capping a hip ridge. Cover the ridge to a distance of about 4 inches to each side—stay within the guidelines—with plastic roofing cement. Press the first long cap shingle in place. Use about 6 nails per shingle. Cover each nail with a little cement. Coat the upper 6 inches of the in-place shingle with cement. Press the following capping shingle an equal distance over the first and keep on going until all the ridges are capped. The end of the last shingle is covered with a short, cemented-in-place shingle.

17

Using Ladders, Scaffolds, Jacks, and Pulleys

LADDERS

If the ladder is going to rest against the side of the building, select a ladder that will permit you to stand 3 feet short of its top and still comfortably reach as high as you need to. If you have to stand higher than this on any ladder, the ladder is dangerously short for the job.

If the top of the ladder is going to rest against the lower edge of a roof, select a ladder that is long enough to extend at least 1 foot above the roof's edge when it is properly positioned at an angle to the building. A shorter ladder is dangerous.

When the top of the ladder is going to rest against aluminum siding, cover the top end of the ladder with a cushion or place a smooth board between the ladder ends and the metal.

When the lower end of the ladder rests on a concrete or a similarly hard smooth surface, tie the bottom end of the ladder to a stake or wedge it in place so that it cannot slip.

To raise a ladder into position, push one end against the side of the building, then lift the ladder over your head as you walk toward the building. If the ladder is so heavy you have difficulty lifting it, get help. If there is a wind, get help. Do not try to do it alone.

When the ladder is in position and you are climbing it, keep yourself fairly upright. Keep your feet near the ends of the rungs. Do not jump when coming down. Step carefully, slowly, and lightly.

When you are working on a ladder, never lean out to one side. Doing so can push the ladder out from under you. When bringing a load of materials up to a roof, be extra careful transferring the load from your shoulder to the roof. Pushing the weight rapidly onto the roof can push you and the ladder away from the building.

Lowering a ladder. Remember that it is much more difficult to control a ladder when lowering it than when lifting it into position. If you had difficulty getting the ladder up by yourself, be certain to get help lowering it. There aren't many shorter routes to rupture than fighting a falling ladder.

To lower a ladder safely, lift the ladder and slowly move the bottom end of the ladder out and away from the building as far as

The safe and proper way to remove a ladder from the side of a building.

you can without the ladder falling down. Then get beneath the ladder, hands upstretched overhead. Take hold of the ladder and gently push it away from the building. As you do so, move your hands quickly up the rungs toward the building until you reach the ladder's balance point.

When you are lowering a two-section ladder, tilt the ladder a little away from the building. Release the safety catches. Pull up a bit on the rope then slowly release it to let the top half come down. Then get behind the ladder and lower it as just described.

SCAFFOLDS

You can rent scaffolds or you can make your own.

The rented type consists of welded-pipe U frames that nest one into the other to reach any height you are willing to stack them. Individual U sections are joined to parallel sections by strap iron braces held in place by wing nuts. You stand and work on construction planks laid across a pair of frames. There are also half frames, which hook into the sides of the U frames. These hold a single plank and permit you to stand and work at half the height of the full U frame.

There isn't much to assembling U-frame scaffolding. Just make certain you have the braces and wing nuts and that the welded-in-place bolts haven't been broken off before you drag the frames out of the rental shop. Without braces the frames won't stand up a moment.

Construction planks. Sometimes called building planks or just plain planks, these are 2 × 10s made of spruce. They are very difficult to break across, which makes them very safe for this purpose. Ordinary lengths of fir and poplar are easily broken in half, which is why many state and local community building departments make the use for scaffold purposes of any other wood but spruce illegal.

Wooden scaffolds. These are quickly made from 2 × 4s, 1 × 8s, and planks. Start by making two H frames using a pair of "clean" 2 × 4s for each leg. Inspect each 2 × 4 carefully to make certain it has no knots and no thick sap lines. Space two of the 2 × 4s about 30 inches apart and parallel. Cut two pieces of 1 × 8 roofers (yellow pine) about 4 feet long. Place one board atop the other and nail the pair across the 2 × 4s at a distance above their ends equal to the desired plank height above the ground. Use three or four 10-penny common nails at each joint. You can use a single, clean 2 × 6 in place of the roofers. But don't use a length of 2 × 4 in this position. It isn't strong enough.

To raise the scaffold into position, nail the end of a long 1 × 8 to the side of one of the 2 × 4s with a single nail. Then lift the H frame up, using the 1 × 8 board to help you if the frame is very tall. With the frame vertical use a stake, rock, or friend to hold onto the 1 × 8. Now lift the second frame into position the same way. This done, nail the lower ends of the 1 × 8s to the lower ends of the 2 × 4s and drive a nail through the 1 × 8s where they cross. Go to the other side of the H frames. Fasten two more cross 1 × 8s to the vertical 2 × 4s. Now you have two vertical H frames with crossed braces holding them vertical and separated. Go to either H frame. Nail a pair of diagonal braces onto it, keeping the tops of the 1 × 8 braces below the cross board that supports the planks. Do the same to the other H frame.

If the scaffold is on firm, level soil, fine. Let it be. If the soil is soft and wet or likely to become soft and wet, slip a 1 × 6 or larger board beneath each pair of legs. A single toenail through the 2 × 4 and into the 1 × 6 will prevent the scaffold from moving off the board.

If the supporting earth is sloped, use the same supporting board arrangement and then slip as many additional boards as necessary beneath the supporting 1 × 6. Do not simply raise the scaffold leg onto a brick or stone. It will eventually move off.

Now you can slide the construction planks in place and work

on the scaffold. It will safely hold two men and a few hundred pounds of materials. Make certain the plank ends overhang their supports by at least 1 foot.

Ladder hangers. Sometimes called ladder scaffolds, these are strap iron triangles that literally hang from the rungs of a ladder. To use them, you position two ladders some distance apart and at a safe angle against the wall. The hangers are then hooked onto rungs, and the planks are slipped through the triangles.

Ladder scaffolds are useful but somewhat inconvenient because their use is limited to where you can properly position two ladders, and your distance from the wall on which you are working cannot be varied very much. Still, they provide a platform that is easily erected and removed.

Roof jacks. Sometimes called roof scaffolds and roof hangers, they are manufactured in two general designs. One looks much like an oversized letter *J*. The upper portion has a hole that is hooked over a nail driven into the roof deck. The lower portion engages the width of a 2 × 6. Naturally, two of these jacks are required. This design is most useful on a moderately sloping roof where you want backup protection, just in case your shoes slip, and something to hold roll roofing and other material while you work.

Whereas the J type holds a 2 × 6 flat against the roof, the bracket type supports a horizontal platform that can consist of one 12-inch-wide board or two 6-inch boards. The second design is almost always used on steep roofs.

Always use a 10-penny common or larger nail. One for each jack is sufficient, but make certain you drive the nail into a rafter, not merely through the roof sheathing. And drive the nail into the deck until its head almost touches the metal.

When you no longer need the jack at that position, do not remove the nail and use it again—it will have been weakened. Either remove it and discard it, or drive the nail home.

Using a roof jack.

You can use ordinary lumber, preferably fir, for the roof jack planks. But do not use any plank longer than 10 feet or thinner than a nominal 2 inches. And use only clean lumber—no knots, no thick sap lines.

PUMP JACKS

Sometimes called pump brackets or pole jacks, pump jacks are mechanical arms that are fitted over a pair of 2 × 4s that have been nailed together to make a 4 × 4. These jacks can be raised and lowered on their supporting 4 × 4 by pumping their control arms up and down.

For greatest safety it is best to use only single lengths to make the 4 × 4s that carry the jacks and the planks. Since you may require 2 × 4s as much as 30 feet in length, single lengths can be very expensive. Therefore, most mechanics make their 4 × 4s from a number of pieces. There is nothing wrong with this if you use only clean fir and stagger the points by at least 6 feet. Use

Erecting a pump-jack scaffold.

  A. One man lifts while the other holds the end of the 4 x 4 in place. *Courtesy Buy Rite Siding, Inc.*

  B. Each of the two metal brace arms clamped to the top of the 4 x 4 and nailed are also nailed to the building.

  C. Pole and pump jack in place. Here it supports an aluminum "plank," which naturally is much stronger than a wooden plank. *Courtesy Buy Rite Insulation, Inc.*

C

10-penny common nails to join the 2 × 4s. Drive the nails into the wood at an angle; stagger them in the width of each side and from one side to the other. One nail for every lineal foot of the composite 4 × 4 is plenty. Pound the nailheads below the surface of the wood or the jacks may "hang up" on them.

Prepare the strap iron braces (two for each pole) that fasten the top of the pole to the building and the necessary 10-penny nails. Secure a ladder that will enable you to reach as high up on the building as the poles will.

Nail the ends of two straps to one pole—one nail in each hole will do. Raise the pole into a vertical position alongside the building. Spread the two straps and nail their ends onto the building. Use a spirit level and make certain the pole is in a nearly vertical position. Do the same with the other pole. Place the planks across the jack arms, making sure the planks extend 1 foot or a little more beyond the arms.

Now step onto the planks and work one pump until you have raised that end of the scaffold a few inches. Go to the other jack and pump some more. Repeat until you are up where you want to be.

Remember, the jacks are plenty strong so long as they are loaded vertically. Don't lean out; don't jump up and down. Don't push against the building, and don't let the scaffold go more than a few inches higher at one end than the other at any time.

PULLEYS

The most arduous task in roofing is to bring the shingles and other materials up onto the roof. The hard way is to carry the materials up on your shoulder while you climb a ladder. The much easier way, certainly on yourself, is to have a helper pull the material up to you with the aid of a rope and pulley.

Get a construction pulley made for hoisting and a manila rope ½ inch thick and a dozen feet longer than twice the distance to the roof. Provide a supporting arm by nailing a 2 × 6 inch plank to two 2 × 4 legs. Make the 2 × 6 at least 10 feet long. The 2 × 4s are most convenient when they are about 5 feet long.

On a new, uncovered roof you can nail the wood tripod you have made directly to the roof. On a shingled or otherwise finished roof, hold the end of the 2 × 6 down with a bag of sand or a number of blocks of concrete. Nail the ends of the 2 × 4s to a 1 × 6 board which is held in place by more concrete blocks.

The pulley is hung from the end of the 2 × 6 with several turns of heavy galvanized wire. Thread the rope through the pulley. Signal your helper on the ground to tie a shingle bundle to the rope and haul away.

18

Safety

There is nothing inherently dangerous about siding or roofing a house. But you will be working above the ground, you may be working with a power saw, and you may be carrying fairly heavy weights up a ladder.

CHECK YOURSELF FIRST

Wear suitable clothing—nothing dangling or hanging that may catch on something. Wear work shoes with rubber bottoms; laced, ankle-high lineman's shoes that have rubber soles are best.

Don't work when you don't feel well or you are tired. It is when you are in either condition that accidents are most likely to happen. If you are unaccustomed to the work, rest before you get tired. If the day is hot and sunny, wear a hat and drink lots of liquid. Stay away from beer and other alcohol. A couple of drinks on the patio won't do you much harm, but up on a roof a couple of drinks can kill you.

Be careful going up and down ladders. This is where much of the falling takes place. People get careless. Be especially careful carrying a load of shingles up a ladder. It is very hard work and will put a heavy strain on your heart. Break the bundles in two. Rest a few minutes at the top of the ladder each time you go up with a load whether or not you feel you need to rest.

DON'T WORK IN INCLEMENT WEATHER

When you are uncomfortable, you fail to take the precautions you would ordinarily take. When the roof is slippery or icy, the danger of injury is multiplied many times over. When your hands are cold, you cannot grip your tools or the ladder properly. A falling hammer, for example, can do a lot of harm.

LADDERS

Inspect every ladder thoroughly before you climb it the first time. If it has been painted (which should never be done), make certain the wood hasn't rotted beneath the paint. If it is of metal, make certain the metal hasn't been badly bent then straightened out at some prior time. Bending and straightening weakens the metal greatly.

Do not use an extension ladder that has to be extended more than 80 percent of its length. For example, an extension ladder consisting of two 10-foot sections should never be extended beyond 16 feet. If you extend the individual ladders farther apart, you are asking too much of the clips that hold them together in the middle.

Make certain the ladder's feet are on a firm, level surface. If the earth is not level, place a plank underneath the ladder. Nail cleats to the plank so that the ladder won't slip. If the ladder is on damp soil, stand on the lowest rung to see whether or not the ladder will sink into the soil.

Make certain the angle of the ladder against the building is correct. If the ladder is too steep, it has a tendency to swing away from the building. If the angle is too close to horizontal, the load on the ladder is dangerous. Generally an angle of about 22 degrees to the side of the building is best.

When the top of the ladder is placed against a scaffold, tie the end of the ladder to the scaffold so that there is no chance of the ladder sliding sideways.

WORKING ON SCAFFOLDS

Walk slowly and carefully. Do not jump up and down. The board that supports your steady weight may break when you jump on it: The force of the downward motion multiplies your weight many times over.

Do not lean over the edge of the scaffold. Your leaning weight may move the frame sideways. Keep the scaffold clean of tools and materials. If you have to have material up next to you, keep it orderly so that there is no possibility you will trip over it.

WORKING ON ROOFS

If you are working on a roof scaffold, which consists of one or more boards placed across roof jacks, make certain the boards do not have any knots. Do not use boards more than 10 feet long and make certain the jacks are at least 1 foot in from the end of the boards. Take the time necessary to find solid wood into which to drive the 10-penny common nails on which the roof jacks hang. Take the time necessary to make certain the jack hooks over the nail.

Keep the roof immaculate. Do not let grains of stone from the surface of the roofing collect. Do not let any tool remain on the roof. Always hook all tools into your belt. Wear a carpenter's nail apron so that there will be no chance that you may forget and leave nails on the roof. Keep all roofing materials uproof from yourself on the areas where you will have no need to walk.

If all this appears to be somewhat ridiculous, remember, step on a nail, a loose shingle, shingle granules, or a tool—and you will slide down the roof.

SAFETY LIES IN FEAR

Don't fight your fear. It is natural and normal to be afraid of heights. Do not try to diminish this fear because it is fear that will keep you careful and cautious. When this fear goes, when you become so acclimated to the height that you forget it and act as if you are on the ground, the chance of an accident increases tremendously.

So work slowly and cautiously and, as old roofers say, "Never step back to admire your work."

Index